Stuart

THE
Mustang
Wranglers

THE Mustang Wranglers

CURLY R.V. GUNTER

FIFTH
HOUSE
PUBLISHERS

Front cover painting, *The Mustang Wranglers,* by Valerie Hinz
Cover design by NEXT Communications Inc.

The publisher gratefully acknowledges the support received from The Canada Council and the Department of Canadian Heritage.

Printed in Canada by Best Book Manufacturers
97 98 99 00 01 / 5 4 3 2 1

CANADIAN CATALOGUING IN PUBLICATION DATA

Gunter, R.V. (Russell V.), 1897–1980

The mustang wranglers

ISBN 1-895618-91-6

1. Horse industry – Canada, Western – History.
2. Horsemen and horsewomen – Canada, Western – History.
I. Title.

FC3209.R3G85 1997   636.1'009712   C97-920008-3

FIFTH HOUSE LTD.
#9 – 6125 – 11th Street SE
Calgary AB Canada T2H 2L6

Contents

....

To my wife, Lena,
my children, Jean, Marlene, and Jack,
and to all my grandchildren

Map by Brian Smith/Articulate Eye
Note: scale is not exact

The author. *Courtesy Marlene Davidson*

Preface

I WROTE *THE MUSTANG WRANGLERS* BECAUSE I WANTED TO keep alive the memory of a great adventure. This true story describes the experiences of a wrangler crew, of which I was foreman, and our fourteen-hundred-mile journey through vast prairie and forest with a large horse herd. The drive began at Val Marie, Saskatchewan, near the Montana border, and ended at Pouce Coupé, in the Peace River country of British Columbia. It was an experience never to be forgotten or duplicated, as large horse herds in Saskatchewan are a thing of the past.

Since this trip, in 1931, many changes have taken place in the area we travelled through. Roads and crossings run through this country now, and large bridges have replaced the old wooden ferries. In those days, Dawson Creek was little more than a country post office, and settlers were just beginning to take up claims in the wild, unsurveyed country. Today, Dawson Creek is a flourishing city just a few miles from Pouce Coupé. Highways have been built through to the coast, connecting the Peace River block with Vancouver. The Alaska Highway has put this corner of the world on the map, and its many natural resources have proven its worth.

It is my hope that this story will be of interest to today's youth, as well as to the pioneers of my century.

(CURLY) RUSSELL V. GUNTER

Drought,
Depression,
and No Grass

F OR THE THIRD YEAR IN A ROW, THE SETTLERS OF SOUTH-
western Saskatchewan were feeling the effects of drought. To
top this off, a world-wide depression had gotten a stranglehold, and
all agricultural products sold for far below the cost of production.
The summer of 1931 would go down in history as the driest year on
record since the early homesteading days. Chinook winds blew all
summer, and clouds of black dust often darkened the sky. Farmers'
crops were cut off by blowing topsoil, and pastures were covered
until some looked like summer fallow.

Drought and depression were hard blows to these early settlers,
but even these disasters did not steal the smile from their faces.
These homesteaders and ranchers, the salt of the earth, had made a
beginning on the old buffalo ranges, miles away from a railroad,
and, often, miles from their nearest neighbours. They knew about
hardship.

In the ranching districts, centred near the watershed from the
international boundary to a few miles south of the Weyburn-
Lethbridge railroad, it had not rained for about eighty days. The sky
would darken, but the clouds carried sand instead of rain. The heat
was terrific.

The countryside was badly overgrazed. The grass on the ranges struggled to stay alive but could not grow—it was trampled by ·thousands of hooves. Winter ranges were already being used for summer pastures. The thousands of horses owned by farmers and ranchers would live the summer, but there would be no winter ranges and no surplus winter feed. Stockmen were calling meetings to decide what could be done to improve conditions. Farmers' milk cows were at stake, and wherever grass could be found, it was used to save them from starvation. Pastures were covered with summer fallow, and many horse ranchers had moved their horses to parts unknown, where drought had not scarred the land with its ugly claws.

The country's water table had fallen by several feet, and springs in the hills failed to supply much water unless they were scraped out and deepened. The sloughs were dry, and many creeks were little more than a trickle. The situation was serious.

The folks at the G Half Diamond ranch, located in the Val Marie district, seventy miles south of Swift Current, had big notions of starting a new horse ranch in the Peace River area of northern British Columbia. Here, drought was supposed to be unknown. Other neighbours were throwing their horses into the herd and were ready to look for new stamping grounds. It would mean a fourteen-hundred-mile drive through heat, dust, and unknown country. Half the journey would be on an Indian trail through the northern forests of two provinces, where much of the country was unsurveyed.

The stories told about the mosquitoes of the North were frightening, but true. The ranchers also had to consider the scarcity of water for the horse herd along the way. The riders who would go on this drive needed to be tough, willing to ride broncs, pull muskeg, and fight the elements in an unknown land; there could be no weaklings or inexperienced men who might quit when things got rough. They had to volunteer willingly and crave adventure.

The ninth of July was set as a starting date. There was much to do before then. A roundup wagon had to be prepared for the trip, with canvas, cupboard room, a stove, and water barrel; horses had to be rounded up from across four townships of hills and valleys in order to separate the trail horses and get them together for the drive. More saddle horses were needed for the long days ahead, and even more horses to be broken to saddle. It would be a mad rush to meet the deadline.

The cowboys who volunteered for this trek were all friends and neighbours well known to me. I, Curly Gunter, of the G Half Diamond ranch, was elected as crew foreman. Whalebone, Blake Powell, had volunteered to do the cooking. Big George Patineau was to drive a wagon loaded with a mower, some harness, oats, rope, corrals, and miscellaneous articles too numerous to mention. He was also supposed to help the cook when necessary. Little Bill Colby and Rawhide, Eddy Torrance, were to ride with me, making three riders and two wagon men.

Blake Powell loved the cowboy life, and for many years that was his trade. He had ridden for horse ranchers and cattle spreads and had built a small horse ranch of his own on the watershed, about thirty miles south of Ponteix. Blake was not afraid of work; he would always do his share or more. Fear was something he seldom thought of. He was not a fancy rider on a bronco, but a mighty tough boy to throw. His endurance was something for a man to be proud of. He weighed around 180 pounds and looked like he might have been a fairly handsome chap before he had abused himself with so much hard living on the range. He was a fierce storyteller—when his listeners were willing to listen—and was a good-hearted, healthy man, tough enough to earn the title of Whalebone. His disposition was quite different from the rest of our crew. If he liked you, he was a true friend. If he didn't, his mind ran on one track only, and his memory was like an elephant's. He wasn't the world's best chef, but he fed us plenty and was always on the job doing his best. He could turn his hand to any kind of ranch work and never complained about the day being too long. Blake was in his late thirties. So far he had not married, although he told the crew that he had big intentions of doing so. He felt sure he could build a log house big enough for two, and shoot moose, bear, and small game. He planned to start a ranch in the new frontier, east of the Rocky Mountains in British Columbia. He was well acquainted with all the boys in the party, who were determined to make this drive.

George Patineau was a large man, weighing about 225 pounds. He was not fat, but was broad and tall. He was a very jovial fellow, always seeing the sunny side of life. A bachelor, he had a huge appetite and a wonderful desire for fun. Big George was a French Canadian who had many friends and a talent for making a new one whenever he met a stranger. If he was your pal, he would be willing to die for you. He was as honest as men come and loved a party. He had been very active in his youth but was getting up in years, at age sixty-three. He saw no harm in a good joke and did not dislike the taste of beer, wine, or a stronger drink on occasion. In addition to his affection for people, he had a great love for his horses and his dog. He was willing to take them to wherever food could be found, regardless of the wagon ride he must endure through heat, rain, mud, hail, and mosquitoes. George was not a bronco buster as cowboys go, but had been a horseman all his life and had always been able to break his horses to harness for farm work. If one of his animals was sick, he would spend his last dime to make it well. In 1931, George was a strong, active man, a man to ride the river with.

Billy Colby was a young man of seventeen years. He had been raised on the C3 ranch in our community by his uncle and aunt, the Clarks. He had ridden good ponies since he was big enough to mount one, and the C3 had raised many Kentucky bronc horses that were wild and fast. Billy was a slim, small lad for his age and got the name of Little Bill. He had a string of good ponies. Some were getting old, and he had picked young horses to replace them. He loved a good horse, but did not enjoy riding a bronco. Little Bill was a schoolboy pal to Rawhide, and they were together whenever possible. Billy was a natural entertainer—it seemed once he heard a song on a record, the tune and words stuck with him. He could sing and play instruments in a good old-fashioned western way. He was truthful, honest, and seemed to have a way with the younger folks. This youngster was a true gentleman in all respects.

Eddy Torrance was also a lad of seventeen years. His black curly hair and heavy eyebrows matched his iron muscles, which seemed to be made of rubber. He weighed only about 150 pounds but seemed to have the strength of a giant. He was honest, truthful, and as willing as could be found. Eddy was raised in the hills, east of Val Marie, on a stock ranch and had gained a great deal of experience with horses while going to school and back. Sometimes he rode eight miles or more to school. In those days, he would average about two new horses a week, and his experience in horse breaking soon grew. The name Rawhide was very appropriate. In the Coriander country that was Ed's home, he had been bounced off a horse in nearly every section of the district, but never seemed to get hurt. He didn't know the meaning of fear. The fact was, he loved to ride a horse, wild or otherwise. From boyhood, he had been his dad's right-hand man, as he was the only son on the ranch, and could hold a branding iron at an early age. He was a boy who was well known and well liked.

It is hard to write about one's self without sounding like a braggart, so these remarks are shorter than those about the rest of the crew. In 1931, I was in my midthirties. My experience with horses and cattle came from years of working with them. My brothers and I had run herds on the open range, before the country was fenced, in the Val Marie district, near Hillandale, Saskatchewan. We were obliged to learn to rope and ride, or we would have been forever put afoot in the hills. My parents, Tom and Elizabeth Gunter, had named me Russell, but as soon as I could walk, my dad and neighbours called me Curly, owing to my curly hair. The name Russell was soon forgotten, and Curly stuck for the balance of my days. I was married, with a wife and young daughter to leave behind when we headed out for this long drive to British Columbia.

I was given responsibility for a crew of men and a large herd of horses, with very few dollars in my pocket. But I knew the crew was made up of men who could depend on one another, regardless of what turned up. This, alone, gives a family feeling. It was a good start.

The
Cowboys'
Farewell

....

THE ROUNDUP WAS ABOUT FINISHED. THE GATHERED horses were held in a two-section field at Whalebone's small ranch in the hills of the Broncho district. The wagons sat ready in his corral.

July was hot for bronco busting, hot for riders and horses alike. Rawhide, Whalebone, and I had been roughing out broncos for a few days, from daylight until dark, trying to saddle break another ten head for the road. The dry corral dust would near choke a fellow, and the only moisture we seemed to have ran out of our eyes.

One nice, upstanding, red-and-white pinto gelding, wearing the G Half Diamond brand, caught Whalebone's eye. He wanted to top this one himself and have some pictures taken.

Pinto, for all his beauty, was a fairly rough character. By the time he had been sacked out and his tail pulled short, the horse knew what he would do with Whalebone. Pinto weighed about 1,150 pounds. He was in good flesh with bulging muscles above nice clean bone in his legs. He had power, action, and plenty of nerve. Whalebone did not intend to let Pinto buck if he could help it and soon had the horse halter-broken, so he would follow him around the corral without a lead rope.

"Boys," said Whalebone, "Pinto will be a top horse for any man. All he needs is a gentle hand and a little encouragement. When I put my saddle on his back today, I'll show you fellows something here. I think I'll ride him this afternoon to see my girlfriend and bid her goodbye."

I began to laugh. "Now, boy, I'd advise you to take my old Captain horse and be safe. I always hate to see a guy walking home in the morning with high-heeled boots, especially when we have another hard day's work tomorrow."

Whalebone snorted, "Don't worry about me, Curly. I'm an old hand."

Rawhide grinned a little and said, "I hope you're old enough."

"I hope you're not too old," I said, still laughing.

Whalebone placed a heavy hackamore on Pinto's head and stroked his white face, and ears and neck. He talked to him lovingly, as if he were the girlfriend who was on his mind. His new saddle was on top of the pole fence in the round corral, ready to be used for the first time.

Whalebone was chewing tobacco with extra energy. He got his saddle on Pinto, but when he tightened the cinch, the pony squealed like a pig at a slaughter house and pitched high and crooked. Whalebone caressed him and cussed him a little, settling him some, then finally climbed on his back. He whirled him around until the horse seemed to enjoy it.

"Curly, keep up a saddle horse so you can ride with me to the top of the hills after supper. I'm going to take Pinto for a good ride," Whalebone shouted.

The air had cooled, and the sun was high in the western sky when we went back to the corral. I led my saddle horse inside so I could ride out with Whalebone when he was ready. Little Bill and Rawhide sat on the top rail of the corral to watch the show. They straddled the fence and were betting their small change—one bet his money on the horse, while the other bet on the rider. They were laughing and talking when Whalebone climbed into his saddle.

Before the rider's feet were in the stirrups, Pinto exploded with a vengeance. Inside of three crooked buck jumps, as high as a man's head, the horse set across the corral, hitting the fence straight on as though he hadn't seen it. He broke three poles and then swapped ends, while Whalebone sailed over the fence like a blanket. The dust whirled inside the corral as Pinto tried to loosen the new saddle.

Through all the dust, the boys on the fence could hear Whalebone cussing all pintos for being so dang blind that they couldn't see a fence six feet high. Whalebone's clean trousers were soiled, and he had a foot-long tear in one pant leg. The cowboy was limping and cussing, while the boys on the fence laughed as if they had been watching a circus. This kind of excitement was not an everyday occurrence.

There was not enough time to gentle all the horses, so we promised ourselves we would work them out later in some corral along the way, or in some stock yards we might pass. We were leaving tomorrow for British Columbia.

A farewell party was held on the evening of July eighth, at Little Bill's home. My brothers, Bill and Lorne, had helped on the roundup and were there with many friends to wish us luck on our long trek to northern British Columbia. Little Bill, who had a good voice and could sing by the hour, could also play a violin and guitar; his sister could entertain, too. Together, they were the life of the party.

Little Bill's sister made up a program for the evening by calling on many people from the crowd. We had a hearty send-off with recitations, speeches, songs, step-dancing, mouth-organ playing, and "what can you do?" At one point, I was called on to tell the crowd how I felt about being responsible for the crew and such a large horse herd.

When I took the stand, I said, "I want to thank the crowd for such a nice evening, and I want to thank my brothers, Bill and Lorne, for gathering all the horses. I have never felt more lonesome in my life than at this moment, for my wife, Lena, and three-year-old daughter, Jean, are not at the party. They've gone to live with my wife's parents, near Ponteix, until I return. I won't see them for months, and already I feel homesick.

"I am expecting a great deal from the boys in the crew, but would never ask them to do anything I would not do myself. I'm

Jean and Lena Gunter. *Courtesy Marlene Davidson*

satisfied that the crew is of top calibre and hope they are satisfied with me. It's likely the cook will get a very rough deal trying to feed us all, three or four times a day, between stops and starts on the road, but I expect support from everyone. Driving a horse herd is far different than being on a cow roundup, for we won't be travelling before daylight in the mornings. When our horses have grazed their breakfast, away we'll go until we find another campsite and they want to graze again. There will be times when we'll all be tired, as we may travel forty or fifty miles some days to find enough water. Other days, we may only travel a few miles."

I smiled and said, "Our crew are all gentlemen, and we expect to be treated as such. We'll treat the other fellow like we would want him to treat us, but if anyone comes looking for trouble, then he better come prepared because we'll never run away." With this, the crowd cheered so long and loud that I said "Thank you" and sat down. It was well past midnight, and the party broke up soon after. The boys went to their tent to sleep and ease their rope burns and aching joints.

The next morning was hot, but we were ready to start. The horse herd was to be moved northwest, through the hills and valleys, to a branch of the Snake Creek near the north end of the G Half Diamond range.

Whalebone and Big George moved away shortly after breakfast, while Rawhide, Little Bill, and I did plenty of hard riding to gather the horses. This field of horses had ranged in many different bunches all summer and were hard to handle in one group. When they were turned out into open country, they tried to scatter, and ran like antelope. But we held them together, and galloped for miles. When we caught up with the chuck wagon somewhere near Hoyle school, we stopped for a drink of water from the barrel. No dinner was had until five o'clock that evening when the chuck wagon, with four horses strung out, came bobbing along over a prairie hill and halted near the source of Snake Creek. We all had a big appetite for our first feed on the trail.

The riders got Whalebone's horses unhitched, unharnessed, and turned into the bunch as quickly as possible, then helped unload the stove. Whalebone soon had the coffee boiling and bacon sizzling in the pan.

Big George trailed along about an hour later. His big black dog was near choked for a drink. The boys watched the dog lap up water from the creek; he would quit for a second or two and then go right back for more.

This was a sample of the cowboy life we could expect until the horses were trail broken.

. . .

*It had been a hot day in July 1931. We had an early supper.
My dad, W. Owen, brought a team of horses hooked on a wagon
to the door, the family got in, and we were on our way to a farewell party at the Clarks. That was Bill's home. The party was for
the men who were driving a herd of horses up to the Peace River
country, from near Val Marie.*

*When we got there, some of the men were at Blake (Whale-
bone) Powell's corral, breaking a bronc. When it started getting
dark, the men all came into the house, and it was then that the
party started.*

*My dad got out the violin, and my brother John played the
mouth organ. They started dancing waltzes, two-steps, and a
popular dance at that time called the eight-some-reel. There were
four couples in each set. My younger sister and I had to dance,
as there weren't enough women.*

*Fanny was Bill's sister. They were a lively pair, both musi-
cal, and able to play the violin and guitar. They knew all the
words to songs and were very entertaining. She had a program
made out, and anybody she knew that could play, sing, recite, or
step-dance, or whatever, was called out of the crowd to perform.*

*Bill was first. He sang a few songs. Among them were "The
Big Rock Candy Mountain" and "The Chisholm Trail." Then
they called on Curly. He sang a song about Olé Olson, who
came from Norway. I don't know the words, but I can still
remember the tune.*

*Fanny and my sister Annie also sang a few songs. One of
them was "The Red River Valley." A few recited, and someone
did a step-dance. Bill and Eddie Torrance (Rawhide) did the frog-
dance. It's a dance where you take each other's hands and crouch
down and kick your legs forward. We then sang a few tunes all
together that everyone knew, and then it was time for lunch,
which was sandwiches, cookies, and cake that the women had
prepared.*

Mrs. Clark always made big sponge cakes, with thick icing on them. We kids sure enjoyed that. There was a pitcher of home-made lemonade, too.

After lunch, they called on Curly again, as he was the fore-man of the crew and had most of the responsibility for the trip. When he finished speaking, everyone just clapped and cheered.

It was a good party and lasted until well after midnight. Everyone seemed to enjoy themselves. We bid them farewell and wished them the very best on their long journey. Then we all left for home. The men were leaving the next morning.

I imagine it was lonely for Curly and the Clark family, as Curly was leaving his family behind, and Bill had never been away from home before.

The sad part of this story is that Bill never saw his sister Fanny after this. She took very sick all at once. They took her to the hospital and found she had an incurable form of diabetes. She passed away about six weeks later. She was nineteen.

AMY (OWEN) PARRISH,
AGE SEVENTY-SEVEN
MARCH 1996

Little Bill (far left), his sister Fanny, and their uncle and aunt, the Clarks, c1931. Man on right is unknown. *Courtesy Amy Parrish*

We Lose
the Chuck Wagon

THE NEXT MORNING WAS HOT, WITH NO BREEZE, SO THE riders put their jackets, chaps, and slickers in the chuck wagon. It took plenty of time to catch the herd for the day. We had trouble getting the saddle and wagon horses near the wagons and into the rope corral we had set up. When a can of oats could not help us catch any more of them, we had some rope practice and lassoed the balance, then we were on our way.

About two o'clock, Whalebone thought his horses were hungry so he and Big George stopped to feed them some oats from George's wagon, while the two men ate a cold dinner. The wagons were late as they headed toward Number Four highway, following a prairie trail. The trail made a few turns in the hills and somehow the men started heading north, instead of northwest, toward Gouverneur. No one lived along this trail, and the wagons rattled along for miles.

In the meantime, Little Bill, Rawhide, and I scouted around for water for the herd and found a spring that was scarcely flowing. We gave the horses plenty of time to drink, as we were expecting the chuck wagon to come along any minute, and we were all hungry. It was already about four o'clock, but the wagons did not appear.

Little Bill was near famished. "If that outfit doesn't show up here in another fifteen minutes," he said, "I'll ride over to that house, about four miles west of here, and beg a loaf of bread."

I caught a fresh horse from the herd, saddled him up, and rode all the way back to the old campsite where I had last seen the wagons. I did not find any broken wagon nor did I see wagon tracks heading toward the highway. After following a prairie trail north about five miles, I opened some gates in large pastures and inquired of one family who lived nearby if they had seen a covered wagon. The lady of the house said that she had seen two wagons heading north about noon. I thanked her and rode the rough country, across the hills, back to the horse herd. I was feeling very uneasy.

Little Bill and Rawhide were cussing their luck when I returned with no grub and no wagon.

"The wagons are way ahead of us," I said. "They were seen heading north four hours ago. We'd better move the horses to Little Six. Whalebone may be there waiting."

When we arrived at Little Six school, it was past dark. The wind came up strong with a night chill, and we had no jackets. They were lost along with the chuck wagon.

I stayed on night guard all evening. Rawhide and Little Bill hunted the country for Whalebone and Big George until eleven o'clock, but were unable to find them. The boys were discouraged as they turned their saddle horses loose in the herd and gave up. We had no coats, no beds, and no grub or water. The wind was howling. The two young riders crawled into a big culvert under the highway, out of the wind, and went to sleep on empty bellies.

I dozed in my saddle part of the night while my pony grazed, but I woke often enough to know that the horses were all there. I thought of my wife, Lena, and little Jean, and of the good coffee I was used to drinking at home. I thought of the fine meals that Lena made for a fellow she called Curly, and I began to wonder how long it had been since I had felt this hungry.

Early the next morning, I concluded that the outfit could not possibly continue without proper management. From this morning on, the boys must carry a slicker or jacket tied behind their saddles. The chuck wagon must never be left to follow without keeping an eye toward it. Also, I decided that I would give the young riders a chance to change their minds about going farther. I would hear

Curly and Lena. *Courtesy Marlene Davidson*

what they had to say after the chuck wagon was found and their stomachs were filled.

Meanwhile, Big George felt sure that he had driven forty miles leading my big Percheron stallion. But the stallion's lead rope had been rubbing the back wheel of the wagon all day and had frayed through—Old Crusader was a free horse! Whalebone was driving some bronco stock on his chuck wagon and could not let his outfit stand alone to help Big George. But Crusader managed to find a water hole in the dark. At about ten o'clock Big George decided it was best to tie up the wagon, make camp for the night, and wait for sunrise. The two men were tired and very worried.

Daylight comes early in July. Big George and Whalebone had slept poorly. When the sun came up, Whalebone could see Cadillac and another town he thought must be Ponteix. It was about seven o'clock when the cook made his way back to Little Six with Big George trailing close behind.

The two boys crawled out of the culvert when they heard the

chuck wagon. It took very little time to unload the stove that morning. The pile of sourdough hotcakes the crew devoured was something to see—you would have thought we were stockpiling for another day without a feed.

After we were filled with breakfast and had discussed yesterday's events, I said, "Well, boys, how about it. Anyone want to quit and go back home?"

These young riders would cuss some, but never swear. "Not by a damn sight," the two of them declared. "We stay until the bottom drops out."

I got no sleep that morning. The wagon horses were changed for fresh ones, and the saddle horses caught for the day's ride.

Whalebone was full of questions about the road ahead, which ran through farming country. "Where do we camp tonight, Curly?" he asked.

"Well, with good luck, we should make Lac Pelletier. It's a hard drag, but we may have to make it to get water for the stock."

The horses were all filled with grass and water and were bunched up for the day's drive. I held them while the boys helped Whalebone get his fresh team together, hitched, and strung out on the chuck wagon.

Rawhide caught a snorty, half-broken bronc as the lead horse for Whalebone. He just had the team all nicely hooked to the wagon when a car came past on the highway. The lead team gave a snort. Unfortunately, Whalebone did not have his lines, and the leaders swung to the right and began running at about thirty miles an hour.

The runaway team upset the chuck wagon, broke the wagon pole, and nearly split the wagon reach from one end to the other. Rawhide jumped on his saddle horse and raced after them. Soon, he had the snorty lead horse snubbed to his saddle horn.

The wagon was placed on its wheels, the boxes of food picked up, and the bed rolls loaded for another start. This runaway delayed everything, but Big George got some tools and bolts and soon repaired the broken parts.

An unsmiling Whalebone climbed up on the wagon, took a big chew of tobacco, and headed his outfit north at a high lope. The stove lids were bouncing so much that one fell off and rolled away, only to be picked up by a rider and carried on a saddle horse until the chuck wagon was overtaken.

To the north, farming country spread out for miles, and the roads were well graded in most places. The horses did not travel on the gravel highway if the boys could avoid it, but moved along on dirt side-roads as much as possible.

The boys told themselves that a bad start usually ends well, as the old proverb goes. We were all hoping to get the tin edge off the horse herd in a few more days.

An Inspection

W HEN THE OUTFIT CROSSED PIERCE CREEK ABOUT THREE o'clock in the afternoon, we found a trickle of water that was appreciated by the horses. We made camp here, and the crew near foundered on sourdough biscuits.

Later that night, the wagon men chained the wagon wheels in order to get down the terribly steep hill to Lac Pelletier, and we set up the tent in the dark. Although the grass was short here, the big lake contained fresh water, and the boys could fish and swim to their hearts' content. The outfit planned to stay here a day to wash some clothes, have a bath, a shave, and a haircut, and get some rest.

About eleven o'clock the next morning, a car skidded to a stop beside the tent, and a big husky fellow stepped out of the runabout. He was swearing like a madman. "Who's the boss here?" the stranger wanted to know. "This morning, my man reported to me that your horses were in my hay meadow."

"That was a false report," I replied.

The big fellow seemed ready to murder the whole crew as he growled, "They've been in there for two days! I'm a contractor and have over a hundred horses working. I depend on this meadow for my horse feed."

I thought to myself, If I have to fight, any two men would look easier to handle than this young giant. However, with little hesitation, I stepped up to the stranger and said, "Mister, you don't know what you're talking about. Before you go any further, you'd better listen to me for a minute." The big fellow looked surprised and stared right at me.

"Our outfit just landed here last night at midnight, and a man has been on guard ever since," I informed him. "Some other horse outfit was camped by the lake when we got here, but they left shortly after daylight. You can go and look at our herd. One of our boys is up there in the brakes with them. See what he has to say."

The contractor began to cool down some and said, "It's a good job for you fellows that it wasn't my man that came instead of me. He's tough."

"Tough be damned," I replied. "If he ever tries making trouble for any of my boys, he had better be good and tough. We respect other people's rights, but when they don't respect ours, it means plain war!"

The contractor went back to his car, where another big bruiser sat waiting. He said something to him, unlocked the trunk of the car, and brought out a case of beer. "Boys," he said, "I'm satisfied that it wasn't your horses in my meadow." The contractor left the camp a few hours later in a happy state of mind.

Lac Pelletier beach was a summer resort where many prairie folks were in the habit of gathering on a Sunday. Occasionally, some stayed for a week during the summer. Cabins could be rented and meals bought at certain times of the year. Boating, fishing, bathing, and swimming gave pleasure to many, and picnics were held often. At the north end of the lake was a good set of pole corrals, where the annual rodeo was held.

Indian people had been living in the lake area long before the country was surveyed. They were farming and ranching now and had been prosperous, but the drought and depression were affecting them, too. These settlers were great fishermen and owned boats and canoes. Now they could earn some revenue by renting these boats to the holiday crowds.

By evening, the horse herd had become quite a tourist attraction. Little Bill was playing his violin, while sitting straddled on the wagon pole. He entertained us with "Turkey in the Straw," while

Rawhide step-danced beside the wagon, his spurs kicking up little puffs of sand. Whalebone was grinning and stringing a long-winded yarn to some ladies who were anxious to find out how he managed to feed five people and move so far each day. Before long, Little Bill got his guitar and sang several cowboy songs for the crowd. People brought fish to the wagon for a treat and loaned boats to the boys so they could have some fun.

The next day, when the outfit was ready to move across country, the crew asked plenty of questions that I could not answer. Hey Curly, where will our home be tonight? How many miles do we go today? How far will we be from Swift Current? Will we be camped long enough to get into the city and kick up our heels?

"From here north, I don't know the country very well," I replied. "If we're lucky we'll find lots of grass, and I'm sure there'll be plenty of water in the Swift Current creek. I know some old-time ranchers who lived along that creek before the railroad was built. I expect by this time, each creek bend has been ploughed up. It's going to be dark by the time we get there, but let's just hope that tonight when we reach that river, we find some open country away from the farmers. We really are into civilization for a few days. Some of us will have to learn to sleep on our horses before we get to the Saskatchewan River."

When the outfit stopped for dinner, all we had was a dry camp, and the grass was short and scanty. There was enough territory so the horses did not have to be watched much, but there was no water.

We were getting ready to travel again when a car came across country toward the horse herd. When it got closer, the boys counted five policemen, Royal Mounties from Swift Current. All of the crew had heard stories about horse thieves and the consequences. In earlier days, rustlers were hanged with their own catch ropes. In later years, it was jail.

Little Bill whispered to Rawhide, "I know dang well that Curly's no horse thief. I wonder about Whalebone?"

"Do you suppose we have some brands that don't belong?" Rawhide asked nervously.

As the young riders' minds were spinning away, they watched

Mustangs on the trail. *Courtesy Irene Gunter*

me climb down from my saddle horse and lead him toward the police car. This afternoon, I was riding a green-broken buckskin gelding that was fat and sassy. He was a little shy of strangers and hesitated to go closer than forty feet. One policeman got out of the car and came to meet me. He introduced himself and asked if the herd had been inspected for brands and if brand fees had been paid, as it was against the law to trail stock without a permit.

This policeman was a very decent fellow and a gentleman. "No, we have no written permit," I told him. "But two days ago, I had the boys hold the horse herd at Bull Creek, near Cadillac, while I rode to a telephone and tried to have Scotty, the policeman from Ponteix, come and inspect the herd. Scotty said that he was very sorry, but he was just leaving town on a chase and didn't have time to come. He said to have the boys in Swift Current check our brands."

The policeman said, "You've given me a very satisfactory answer, Mister. How would you suggest we inspect the herd without corralling them?"

"If you can ride a horse, we have a gentle one you can use. It would never do for you to drive in there with your car, and you can't get close enough on foot. I have some papers packed away in the cupboard, containing a list of every brand the horses are wearing."

The policeman was past middle age, with grey showing in his hair at the temples. He had been in the police force a long time and was a credit to the men in the RCMP. He said, "Mister, would you just let me look over your brand list. You know, for missing stock. The force is handed a long list of brands to look for. It's not that we want to personally inspect your horses, but it may lead to some brands of lost stock, from a few years back."

I led my horse back a couple of rods and handed his hackamore rope to Whalebone, who was standing beside the chuck wagon with the team hitched, ready to leave for the trail. "Hold Buck for a minute while I dig out our brand list from the cupboard," I said. "Do you suppose Little Bill will loan this gentleman his roan mare to ride? We certainly want a clean slate to begin with."

While the inspector and I walked toward the horse herd, where the boys were waiting, another young Mountie got out of the car and strolled over to the chuck wagon. Whalebone thought this man looked familiar, but said nothing. The buckskin began to fidget and blew his nose at the stranger. The Mountie exclaimed, "What's wrong with that horse? He acts like he's afraid of me. He sure is a pretty animal."

"There's nothing wrong with him," replied Whalebone. "He's not used to a man very much. He belongs to Curly's wife; she rides him all the time at home. He may be a little lonesome for her. Why don't you take him and go help your partner? We're in a desperate hurry to get on our way. We have to find a campground before dark, where there is water and grass. I'm going to get this chuck wagon rolling right away, or the boys will have cold beans again tonight." Whalebone handed the Mountie the buckskin's reins, climbed up on his wagon, and drove away.

Buck blew his nose on the Mountie's uniform and backed away from him, circling as he stepped. The other three Mounties got out of the car. One fellow came to assist his partner. "Ride him, cowboy," he yelled, as he grasped the hackamore rope and braced himself, acting as a snubbing post. Buck quivered and then stood still.

One of the other young officers said, "Up with you, Corporal," as the Mountie tried to step up into the saddle. When the stranger threw his leg over the horse, Buck dropped his head with a snort and jumped from the rider with great force, then suddenly sprung right back and whirled like a top. The corporal sailed on over him into the cactuses. Buck moved away from the startled bunch of boys, kicking up the dust in the dry grass. He was heading back into the herd as if he meant business, expecting protection from the other horses.

The inspector and I were satisfied that there were no brands on these horses that had been listed with the police. I was paying ten cents per head for brand fees, and we were getting acquainted when he asked, "Where do you expect to camp tonight? It's only a nice drive from here to Swift Current, and there is a wonderful place to camp just south of the city. Everybody camps there. You won't be bothered with anything, and you may want to get into town for the evening."

I thanked him for this information and said, "If we don't find something earlier, we'll be in about dark."

The inspector was wishing me luck when suddenly the buckskin horse came running through the herd, bucking and squealing, scattering the horses over about twenty acres.

Whalebone started the chuck wagon toward Swift Current and chuckled like a schoolboy because he had talked the Mountie into riding Buck. It had been a grandstand. Whalebone wondered how many cactuses the lad would have to dig out of his hide from the spill.

"Buck, you old devil," he said aloud, "I knew you could do it. I wonder what Curly will say about this? It sure was a good show while it lasted. Rawhide will soon catch Buck for Curly. Hurrah, you long-legged devil up there on the lead. Swift Current, here we come. There'll be a hot time in the old town tonight."

Night Herding
in the City

THE HORSE HERD WAS BEING HELD IN A BEND OF THE SWIFT Current creek, where the water was clear and running. The riders laid on their bellies and drank, then waited awhile and drank some more.

"You fellows remind me of Big George's dog when he finds a water hole," I told them.

This river bend had only a few acres of grass, but it seemed fairly long. Everyone realized it was no camping spot for a large bunch of horses so I gave orders to search the creek for a few miles, to look for more grass. Little Bill rode up the creek toward the west and Rawhide rode east, looking for a place to settle for the night. Each rider reported the same thing: wheat fields and summer fallow.

The sun was getting low in the west, and every man was hungry. "No use feeding you fellows here," said Whalebone. "Just grab a snack if you're hungry. When we find that good campground beside the city, we'll have pumpkin pie, beer, and maybe ice cream. I'll take in a talkie—they say they have talking pictures now, and I've never seen one. Then, I'll come straight home and Curly can go. I'll herd for a shift if we ever get there. Hurrah, you long-legged devil up there on the lead. Swift Current or bust."

I loped on ahead to locate the campground, following the directions the police had given me. When I reached the place south of the city, I found plenty of room for the chuck wagon, providing the horses were all tied to a wagon wheel.

The creek flats by the railroad tracks were Chinamen's gardens. They were irrigated, with about three cabbages to the yard in rows. Some patches had little fences of barbed wire. The freight yards, close by, were full of freight cars, and some of them moved and squeaked continually.

I circled the south side of the city for a mile or two. Potato patches and vegetables were green and lovely. What water can do, I thought, as I rode back toward the city. But where will we camp tonight?

I decided to ride west a few miles, but I found only summer fallow and grain fields, which were showing the effects of drought. There was no place to hold the horses for the night.

I rode into the city on the west side, looking back occasionally to see how far behind the boys were with the horses. It was dark now, and the sun had set. A big black cloud covered half the sky. The city lights blinked on and off, and the traffic was heavy. Cars honked their horns at me, and my buckskin saddle horse nearly collapsed from fear as I gently spurred him past some dangerous places. Finally, I came to Number One Highway on the north side of the city. Cars were coming and going, and their lights flashed by me. I discovered a piece of grass, a strip between the highway and a snow fence that ran along the railroad tracks. I began to wonder if I would be able to find the outfit again. I kept on riding and discovered that the highway ran one mile west of the city before it crossed the railroad tracks. This strip of ground was a quarter-mile wide at the city and tapered to a point, one mile west, at the crossing. This is it for tonight, I thought. As poor as it is, it will have to do.

I started backtracking, and just as I went over the railroad crossing, I met Rawhide, who was hunting for me. "The only place I could find for the horses is under the city lights on the west side of town," I told him. "I never heard so much noise in my life. People are running around with cars like crazy. Buck is only half as nervous as I am. Too bad we didn't stay at the dry camp and come through here in daylight. Where's the chuck wagon?"

We rode back to find the horse herd, but had not gone more than half a mile when a big clap of thunder cracked and lightning zigzagged through the sky. "It looks like the first rain of the year," I said. "You'll be able to tell your grandchildren about this night if we all come through it safely."

Rawhide and I met the horse herd, not far south of the city. When these broncos went across the railroad crossing, through the freight yards, they acted like a wild bunch from the hills should act. They heard their feet pounding on the planking of the crossings and the steam hissing. They saw the engine lights on the shunting trains. The city lights shone in their eyes. They heard the roar of thunder and saw the flashes of blinding lightning. Automobiles ran among them at the crossings, honking loudly.

It was no wonder that some horses ran down the tracks, to the west, among the box cars. Others wanted to go east, dodging shunting trains. The rest of the herd galloped madly across the wide crossing. After a lot of hard riding in the freight yards, and a little cussing, the scattered horses were turned back into the rest of the herd. The day's work was finished, but the night was yet to come.

The chuck wagon pulled around the slab fence on the north side of the railroad tracks, and I heard Whalebone calling, "Is this the place, Curly?" He stopped close to the fence along the tracks and soon had the tent set up.

The crew was racing the storm. The echo of thunder bounced around over the city, and came back to camp to start all over again. Big George was driving tent pegs with the back of his axe, his dog curled up under the wagon as if it hadn't a worry in the world. Everyone in the crew was hustling.

"Try to catch a good horse for me tonight, right away. I think you'd better get two gentle ones and tie one, all saddled, to the wagon wheel, in case we need it," I told the boys.

I walked around the wagons in the dark. Where's my slicker packed? I wondered. This wind could blow a man down. Do you suppose we'll ever find the bunch of horses in the dark? It's blacker than the inside of a cow, and I'm hungry as the devil.

Whalebone shouted, "How about a cheese sandwich, about a

foot thick, before you go out, Curly? The boys will have a feed in town. We'll see you about midnight, and I'll take over a shift of night herding. I hope there won't be any hail in that storm." Whalebone talked away while I ate a big lunch and the boys brought in two night horses. There were many things on my mind as I ate my sandwich.

"Whalebone, how come you let that stranger fellow have my buckskin horse at noon?" I asked. "He was so jittery and spooky he was hardly safe for a fellow to ride for the rest of the day."

Whalebone took a fresh chew of tobacco and laughed good and loud. "That fellow was no friend of mine, Curly." He explained, "Two years ago over at a Shaunavon rodeo, another fellow, Big Sam, and I tied in the finals. He seemed to be a real good sport, and we agreed to ride again after celebrating with a bottle or two of beer. But my girlfriend saw Big Sam cut my latigo, so it would break when I was riding the bronc. Well, Curly, I worked that big lubber over as best I could. He was tough with his hands, but did I ever give him a spurring. I'll bet the map of Europe is still scratched on his hide. That policeman is the fellow that wanted to lock me up for being drunk. I had to pay a forty-dollar fine! Do you suppose he picked up forty cactuses at noon?" Whalebone was certainly enjoying the joke.

Several times that night, long freight trains rolled westward through the freight yards and along the snow fence. Other trains went east. All of them whistled at the crossings, which were one mile apart. The horses seemed to run all night. Just as they reached the crossing where Number One Highway intersected the tracks, the train would beat them to it. Its whistle frightened them, and they would turn around and race back toward the city lights, only to end up turning around again.

The night at Swift Current was very hard on my nerves, too. About eleven o'clock, that black cloud poured down rain, hail, and sleet, with a driving wind that lasted for two hours. I heard the horses running but could do little more than follow the noise. The only time I could see a horse was when a flash of lightning lit up the sky, then it was pitch dark again. Once, during the night, when I spotted the tent in a big flash of lightning, I called to Whalebone, good and loud, to come and give me a hand. Then I followed the sound of running hooves to the city lights. The horses would spook from the car lights and trains and make another break for freedom. I had never galloped so much in my life as I did that night.

There was a ditch that either drained the highway or the railroad, and I made a mad gallop into this trench twice during the night. Each time, my saddle horse upset completely. By the time the horse and I picked ourselves up, we had lost all sense of direction. The ground was so muddy from the rain that it was not safe to turn a saddle horse.

Whalebone heard me shouting and scrambled out of the tent, yelling, "Curly, you danged old wrangler, where the heck are you?"

But the wind blew his voice right back at him. At this time, I must have been near the west end of the strip of grass because I could not be found. Whalebone called some more and rode around in the dark for half an hour, locating about fifteen horses. But in less than two minutes, he did not know where half of them were.

Could it be possible that Curly has had a lot of trouble? Whalebone wondered. He's probably tried to corral the horses somewhere. If I find him, that's what we'll do. I wonder if the CPR stock yards are locked at night. The cook touched his spurs to his horse and rode slowly toward the city lights.

Soon after, I found Whalebone under a light pole. "I don't know how many horses I have left," I said. "I think I've lost a hundred head. One bunch went east through the city, and if they held their speed, they'd be getting close to Moose Jaw by now. Another bunch was over in the freight yards among the freight cars, dodging and snorting. If we didn't need fresh ponies for morning, I'd say goodbye to these and go to bed."

"Curly, do you think you can drive what is left through there among those freight cars? I'll ride ahead of them. They may follow me, and if they do, I'll open the stock-yard gate and head them inside. How about it? Can you do it?" asked Whalebone.

It was still very dark, and the rain was drizzling down, when we started over the tracks with the horses. Once Whalebone was away from the light pole, I didn't see him again until an hour after daylight. I just trailed after the horses, hoping they were all following Whalebone's horse.

When the rain eased up and daylight began to break, I was on the south side of the city in the cabbage patches with about thirty head of horses. I was trying to move the horses back to the strip of grass when an airplane came sailing close to the ground looking for a landing field. It flew directly over the herd. Once again, I found myself standing still with horses scattering in every direction, and fast. Such things must be why old cowboys learn to cuss.

In the early hours of the morning, everyone in the crew was on a saddle horse hunting for strays. Before the city awoke, the horses were all at the campground again, and the cook was making breakfast.

Breakfast Guests
and Ferrying
Horses

D URING THE SUMMER OF 1931, THE FLAT CARS AND BOX CARS on the freight trains carried far more passengers than the passenger-train coaches. The depression was so general across Canada that most youths were without jobs, and soup kitchens were set up in different cities to help ease the slow starvation facing people who had no way of making a living. Many youths left the east on the top of a freight car or riding the rods, looking for any job that would provide a full belly and a bed. Men of all ages, trades, and professions were looking for work, but very few folks had enough cash to hire help. Although provincial governments passed relief measures, most people did not have the money to buy farm produce. Eggs sold for two to four cents a dozen. But if the unemployed didn't have that much, they couldn't buy.

The boys with the horse herd had not realized when they left home that the depression was so widespread. Now they were wondering if they could sell enough horses for cash to keep the chuck wagon filled with food.

The horse camp had many visitors this morning. There were nineteen extra men, all hungry for breakfast. The fellows riding the freights, from Montreal to Vancouver, thought they had found a gypsy camp. They straggled in, one or two at a time, saying that they were famished and flat broke. Most of these young men had jungled up alongside the slab fence to rest, and the rain had thoroughly soaked them.

The hobos, as they were branded, came marching toward Whalebone's cook stove, where it sat out in the open. "Holy cow," exclaimed the cook, "it looks to me like those fellows think this might be an open-air soup kitchen. What are we going to do about it, Curly?"

"It's a bad thing to be hungry," I replied. "Better give them something."

"I've got twenty pounds of syrup. I could make them some hotcakes and coffee. That should stick to their ribs for a day. Anyone that don't like that, breakfast is over," he said.

Some fellows from Quebec could not speak English. When one came along who could not communicate with Whalebone, he called Big George over to do the talking, as he could speak French. One husky, curly-headed fellow who had slept in the mud could not speak English either, but he could smell hot coffee and followed his buddies.

This curly-headed boy, about nineteen years of age, walked up to Whalebone and showed him where he had taken his belt up two holes. He could put his hands nearly around his waistline. He was wearing a suit coat that was still wet from the storm, and he turned his coat and pants pockets inside out to show us there was nothing in them. Whalebone was frying hotcakes as fast as he could. When Big George came around to the wagon, the curly-headed lad told him that he had eaten only a few times all week. He had had two apples the day before and thought the hotcakes would be his last feed until he reached the coast, unless he was lucky enough to get a job for his board.

This breakfast session could have lasted all day. When Whalebone and Big George got a chance to load the stove and hook their teams to their outfit, several fellows from the hobo gang wanted to come along. They seemed to like the chuck wagon's hotcakes and coffee.

The boys were watering the horses at the Swift Current creek on the northeast side of the city. Many town children had come out here to see the riders and horses, and they all wanted a colt, but they were crowding in so close that the horses became nervous and moved away from the water.

"All right, boys, keep back until these horses can have a drink, and you can have that white colt if you want him," Rawhide told the youngsters.

At once, they moved back and were quarrelling amongst themselves as to who would own the colt. Several battles took place, much swearing, and some crying.

Little Bill said, "Okay, boys, quit your fighting and get busy. The boy who catches the white colt can have him."

Many Swift Current boys were late for school and anything else that morning. Some little fellows ran on foot for miles. When they became short of breath from running, they asked for help.

Rawhide told one young lad, "You need a rope. How're you going to lead a colt home?" Little Bill told another to get some sugar and yet another to put salt on the colt's tail.

By about ten o'clock that morning, the crowd of youngsters had thinned out. Some went away. Others, a little more persistent than most, were still at the chase. Some children had gone home for sugar and salt, while some had a little piece of rope and others had old horse halters. These young folks did not discourage very easily, but they began to think that they could not catch the colt without assistance from us cowboys and our ponies. The language they used when they could not get help from us could not be printed in this story.

After Big George and Whalebone had driven their covered wagons through the Swift Current streets and joined us on the northeast side of the city, Whalebone shouted, "Hey, Curly, which way are we pointing from here?"

"North as we can go," I answered. "We'll hit the Saskatchewan River, as near to the ferry as we can. We should make good time today, the grub box isn't quite so heavy."

Everybody laughed, and I said, "Those poor devils certainly

were hungry this morning. I feel sleepy and a little weary. If these horses weren't so hard to handle, I'd crawl under your tarp and sleep awhile. If we're lucky, maybe we can catch a little shuteye tonight."

Little Bill and Rawhide were trailing behind the horses, while I rode on the lead. When Little Bill asked Rawhide if he had ever seen a ferry before, he answered, "No, I haven't. I don't believe I've even seen a picture of one. The White Mud is the biggest river I can remember seeing."

"Same here," answered Little Bill. "They say the Saskatchewan is a dangerous river and a big brute, too. I wonder how we'll manage to get to the north side. Did you ever ride a horse while it was swimming?"

"I've never crossed more than a big slough and the creeks in the hills," replied Rawhide. "I tried to swim old Baldy in the shallow end of the dam once, but he went plum out of sight. He just kept the end of his nose out of the water. I got my pockets full of water that time."

The next day at noon, the horse outfit was camped beside the Saskatchewan River. From here, we could see the ferry sitting on the far side of the water.

As Big George and Whalebone tied their wagon teams to their wagons, Whalebone began talking to me in a very serious tone. "Curly, you old cowpoke, you're up against something this time. It's a long way across that puddle. How do you intend to put horses on that raft? You know we can hardly put them on a bridge without raising the devil. That old raft would sink if we put a dozen broncs on it. No place to hold these horses, either."

Whalebone rolled a cigarette and lit it. "How're you going to cut out a little bunch from the herd and slip them onto that thing in the water? You can't do it. If you did get them loaded, you could never ride across on the ferry with them to take them off. Do you suppose they could swim that far?"

I was looking at the river and thinking hard. "You'd better have the boys catch you a top saddle horse," I said. "We'll need you badly. I'm going to ride old Captain. If we don't load these horses on that ferry, I'll let some other fellow head the crew."

"That's the spirit!" Whalebone shouted. "I like to hear you talk that way, but you know, your two riders are only seventeen-year-old boys."

"Yup, they're only boys, but what boys they are. One thing, they'll do what they are told to do. If they're riding their best horses, no man ever needed better help. Here's the ferry. Let's talk to the operator."

As we walked toward the man, I said, "You know, Whalebone, our two boys, even mounted on green horses, are better help than many a cowboy on his top horse with a two-hundred-dollar saddle. So relax. If we can't load the ferry here, we may as well go home because we have really big rivers yet to cross."

Three cars drove off the ferry. The passengers stopped long enough to inquire where the horse herd was going. A lady took some pictures of the herd and had us line up on our saddle horses for another shot. "If these pictures turn out, I'll give them to the newspaper in Swift Current," she said. "The *Sun* would like a story about it. I can't see how they missed you when you came through the city."

"We had trouble enough getting past that city without any more scary things happening," I told her.

We watched the cars roll south across the flats of the South Saskatchewan River valley. They boldly climbed the high crooked trail up hills that looked like mountains. We heard the car motors groaning and imagined that we could hear their radiators boiling before they reached the top.

The view east or west along the river brakes was very picturesque. The badlands were so rough that it would bother a pack horse to cross them. The wagons would have to go many miles farther north to bypass such rough country. The river was swift, crooked, and very warm in July. Every day was a scorcher. The big rain at Swift Current hadn't reached farther than a mile or two past the city. The cactuses in this valley were in flower, and some late rose bushes added colour to the scenery. Looking west, I could see a big sandbar in the river.

The ferry operator said, "Yes sir, fellows, if you can load them, I'll ferry them. It's too far to swim, though I have seen stock do it."

"We'll have to use the ferry on the Athabaska, the Smoky, and the Peace," I replied. "If we can't do it now, we won't be able to do it later.

"I'll catch a very quiet horse, put a halter on him with a long rope, and bring him down here beside the ferry," I explained to the ferry operator. "You can stand behind that big wheel and hold the end of the rope. Then we'll cut out a load of about fifteen horses and bring them to this horse. When I tell you to lead this horse onto the ferry, please do so, but keep out of sight if you can."

It was all arranged, and the task began. Inside half an hour, one ferry load was on its way. The horses did a great deal of whinnying and tramping around, but the riders hustled and got the chain hooked on the open end of the scow, and the old ferry pulled loose from where it had grounded.

The sail across the river reminded the boys of their boat ride at Lac Pelletier, but they thought this was much more exciting.

"Curly sure knew what he was doing this time," whispered Little Bill. "He had that old Baldy horse led onto the raft just at the right time."

As Rawhide watched the horses huddle together, he shouted, "Whoopee, this will be the greatest trip of our lives. This is the most exciting cowboy work I've ever had a hand in. When we write the folks at home, this will really be news. I wish my dad could have seen us load this bunch of broncs."

The water was slapping hard against the ferry as it sailed smoothly with the force of the current. The big cables were squeaking and straining from the pull of their load. When the light of the sun was right, the boys could see fish darting about, and they promised themselves a feed of fresh fish for supper.

The first load of horses landed safely on the north bank. The operator unhooked the chain and lowered the platform end of the ferry, where it came to a rest snugly against the ground. The horses scrambled off in a rush, making the ferry jiggle some on the water. They ran along the river, whinnying loudly. Some mares must have had their colts left on the opposite side. The saddle horses stood with the reins down, on the bank where the ferry had been loaded, to await our return. Old Baldy was ferried back for another trip.

The second load was soon pried off the bank. When the ferry was about four rods from shore, my Captain took to the water with his head held high; he must have become confused with so much whinnying from the opposite side of the river. His reins were dragging and his cinch was tight. My sweater was tied behind the saddle. He went straight ahead, swimming high—like a canoe— and soon passed the ferry and landed on the opposite side in record time. The ferry operator had never seen a horse swim so fast.

On the north side of the river, some mares swam back, looking for their colts. On the south side, where the herd was grazing, some colts and yearlings swam halfway across that big river. They became confused by the whinnying horses, turned right around, and swam back. Before they landed, they heard another whinny from the far side and turned around again. That afternoon, some horses swam far enough to almost cross the Saskatchewan River and back. However, old Captain was brought back on the ferry with Baldy, and the loading continued until the last horse was across. Then, with a little help from the crew, Whalebone and Big George hitched their outfits and drove onto the ferry.

The sun was getting low in the west when we made camp along the north side of the South Saskatchewan and settled down for the evening.

The Skunk
and the Rattlers

R AWHIDE AND LITTLE BILL WERE SITTING ON THE RIVER-
bank with a hook and line, trying to catch enough fish for
supper, but they weren't having much luck. I was dog tired and laid
on the ground with my head resting on my saddle and was soon
sound asleep. Big George's dog was curled up beside me, enjoying
the shade of the covered wagon. There was a little breeze blowing
through the wagon's wheels.

When Whalebone had supper prepared, he told Big George,
"It's a shame to wake Curly. He's had very little sleep since we left
home. But when a fellow puts in the hours that he has, he needs to
eat plenty and regular." He continued, "I'd like to have a swim after
supper. We may not see any more water like this."

"When I was a boy," Big George replied, "I used to be a fair
swimmer. Lately, I haven't had much practice. Sometimes I try to
swim in the Snake Creek that runs through my farm. I usually fall
in once or twice every spring when the ice is going out and the water
is bank high. In the summertime, that creek isn't running, and I can
only swim in the big spring-fed potholes. The water isn't always as
warm as I like for swimming. This river is plenty warm tonight, but
it's flowing pretty swift, too."

Big George's dog awoke when Whalebone called, "Come and
get it."

Some of the boys were seated on the wagon pole, and some of us were on the ground with our plates heaped high. The dog began to sniff around the buck-brush patches near the camp. In another minute or two, he had a skunk by the neck and shook it fiercely before he realized what he had in his teeth. This was so near the camp that it would almost make a fellow cry. That poor dog, how he coughed, sneezed, and rolled himself on the ground. Finally, he came running to Big George for help. We all raced away with our supper plates in our hands. Some were swearing a little. Others were telling the dog in a good loud fashion to get away. The big dog landed up in the river, where he spent most of the evening.

The next morning, we had a fairly early breakfast. No one knew where the next camping place would be.

I reported to the crew, "We'll go north until we see the first trail heading west. We better keep in sight of the river, or we may choke to death. From here north, every settler hauls his drinking water from this river. There isn't a well in the whole country. We better lap up enough to soak us up good. I'll bet it's a hundred in the shade this morning, and there won't be any shade until the sun goes down. We should be at Empress in four or five days. Be sure the water barrel is filled before you leave here, Whalebone."

We could hear Whalebone shouting, "Hurrah, you long-legged devil up on the lead. Empress, here we come."

It didn't take long before we were thirsty. Rawhide was riding a bronco, and his breakfast was well shaken down before we had gone half a mile. The half-broken horse was determined to make Rawhide walk. Sweat ran off both of them.

Rawhide was bellowing, "I'd pull leather with both hands if my saddle horn was long enough, but I don't intend to walk very far in this heat! The chuck wagon will never catch us today because these horses seem to be in one heck of a hurry to get to Empress. They'll need water again in two hours."

Little Bill looked into the distance and sighed, "We're headed straight west and are going to run into those mountains before noon. That river is sure crooked—it must twist and turn a whole lot between here and Alberta.

"It looks like Curly is having a lot of trouble trying to hold the horses back. They seem to be running on both sides of him. He's making time this morning.

"I hope my horse doesn't play out. He's been acting like he might be sick."

About ten o'clock, Little Bill looked at Rawhide and complained, "I hate to be put afoot way out here, but my horse has a bellyache. I'm going to turn him loose and wait for the chuck wagon to pick me up. The way the herd is travelling toward the water today, they don't need me chasing them. Tell Curly to take a look at Peanuts when he gets to the river. I hope Whalebone hasn't lost the water barrel, because I'm danged near choked. Good luck to you fellows."

There was no shade, not even a rose bush, for Little Bill as he waited. He curled up in the sun on the prairie, and he began thinking. His mind rambled back to the good spring water that was behind his house. He wondered what his sister had been doing since he left. He would send a long letter, telling all about his trip—if he ever found time to write, and if he didn't get sunstroke.

Somewhere northeast of Cabri, the horses reached the river at a full run. I was galloping ahead with my lariat rope down and whirling the end in a big circle to hold the herd back. It was like being in a stampede of cattle, as they were on each side of me. Nothing on earth would stop their mad rush for water. I was afraid some of them might get lockjaw as they swarmed around me at the river. Rawhide and I laid on our bellies amongst the horses, drinking the hot river water that was flowing east at a furious speed.

As soon as Rawhide quenched his thirst some, he said, "A fellow wouldn't live very long in this weather without water. My tongue was getting thick. I bet Whalebone won't chew much tobacco today because he won't be able to spit."

We watched the horses as they grazed, rolled, and drank some more. The colts were mothering up.

"We won't see Whalebone for two hours," I said. "We must have travelled twenty miles this morning. I sure hope Little Bill found some shade so he doesn't cook himself on the prairie. Peanuts still looks a little dumpish. When the boys get in with the chuck wagon, we'll give him some soda and ginger. He sure is a tough little bronc for his size."

The horses filled with water with no bad results. Some were rolling on the ground to rub the caked sweat from their hides, and others were swimming in the river. All seemed content and happy. The grass was not very long or plentiful, but enough for a noon stop.

While we waited for the chuck wagon, we visited. "We can be very thankful that it cools off in the evening," I said. "August will likely be a hot month, too."

I walked over to my horse and untied my slicker from the back of my saddle, then spread it over some little willows on the river-bank. This made enough shade for our heads, away from the glare of the sun.

I laughed and said, "We'll all look half-Indian before we get these mustangs into northern British Columbia."

I let my mind ponder many things. "From now on," I declared, "we need to watch for snakes. This Saskatchewan River valley has been noted for rattlesnakes. Have you ever seen a rattler?"

Rawhide exclaimed, "Lordy, no. They're bad, aren't they?"

"Yes, they are," I told him. "One thing I can say in their favour is that, as much as I detest snakes, they always warn a fellow once. If we don't heed their warning, then we better look out. It's too dang bad that human beings don't do as much."

Rawhide asked all kinds of questions about snakes and animals. I told him, "The rattler is a very poisonous snake. When you hear a sound like z-z-z, watch where you step. They curl up like a rope coil, with their head in the centre. Their powerful body will give a big heave, throwing their head as high as about half their length."

We joked for a while, then I said, "Now, Rawhide, I could tell you a little story about my experiences with rattlesnakes in Alberta, in the early twenties. Would you like to hear it?"

"Sure, go ahead and tell me."

I grinned. "I suppose you've heard of the old Cameron ranch on the Belly River? I worked there once. I was working with a tall, slim fellow from the state of Washington. He was a reckless devil, something like yourself. He knew no fear and would ride broncs on Sundays for the sport of it. The only time I ever heard him say he was scared was the day we took up a collection among the boys and gave Slim an airplane ride over the Belly River flats. He was very eager for his first plane ride. Have you ever been up in one?"

"No, I never had the price, but I sure would like to. Do you think they'd let me wear my spurs?" asked Rawhide.

We both laughed, and I continued to explain about Slim's plane circling over the brakes of the Belly River. "They were very similar to these brakes beside us. This day, the plane seemed to be running into air pockets. It would drop straight down and then glide on. The river brakes were three hundred feet high, and they were flying away up there above the water. Slim said he was a little scared when that plane began to bob and jump, but he was not afraid of a rattlesnake.

"Slim was raised among rattlesnakes. Often, I saw him spot a big rattler sliding away. He'd run after it with a neck yoke or a long sliver of board. He told me that as long as they're moving, they're harmless. If they coil, look out. The buttons that rattle on the end of their tail are similar to a child's tin rattle.

"One day, we were moving an old pile of lumber onto a wagon. I was at one end of the pile, and Slim was at the other. The lumber was nearly all loaded, just three boards high remained on the pile. When Slim reached his hand beneath the bottom boards and lifted them a foot off the ground, a little snake struck at his hand. If you think I didn't get a shock when I saw what happened, you're wrong. Slim dropped his end of the boards, yelling, 'He got me, Curly!'

"We were working about twenty miles from the town of Taber, Alberta. The only car for miles was a Model T Ford belonging to the ranch foreman. On ranch roads, twenty miles to a doctor for a snake bite, in a Model T, can be a mighty long way. The foreman was called and preparations were made to rush Slim off to the doctor. The foreman said, 'If he struck you, Slim, it will be swelling in a few minutes.' I began to examine his hand for the scratch of a fang and discovered a large sliver that he got when he dropped the board.

"I can still see that little snake coiled up beside the board. It didn't take long to fix him. He was so young that he had no rattlers, just one button on his tail. I've been told that those are the most dangerous of all—they can't rattle to warn a fellow, but their poison is just as potent as an old one."

Then it was back to business. I explained the route we would follow. "Empress is a good town. It's situated in a point of land where the Red Deer River joins the great South Saskatchewan. Both rivers are large. When they join, you can see very little difference in size, but it must be at least twice as deep. At one time, this part of the world was considered rattlesnake country."

Rawhide wanted to know if it was ranching country all along this river.

"In earlier days, it was famous for big ranches," I told him. "The old 76 ranch has its first Canadian ranch between here and Empress. They irrigate big hay meadows, so we may see something nice and green before too long."

Bronco Busting
by the
Saskatchewan

T HE NEXT DAY I TOLD THE CREW, "I KNOW AN OLD COWBOY
who lives up this river. I believe he's in charge of a community
pasture, a fairly big one. I think the ranch is near the town of Lacadena.
If we can find Cowboy George, we'll have the sleep of our lives."

The weather continued scorching hot, and the outfit had to keep
going back to the river for water. The horses were putting on many
extra miles but could not go very far in the heat without a drink.

One Sunday afternoon, we stopped for a little breather. From a
nearby pinnacle, we could see far into the distance. Here, on this
high point, a slight breeze found us, and we were making the best
of it. We let our eyes roam over the big valley below and miles away
to the west. Along the river, we could see patches of brush in many
of the river bends. Perfect range country, I thought. Plenty of shelter,
grass, and water. Some of the best range country in the world.

From the high peaks of the river brakes, I could see a good set of
stock corrals and some other small buildings several miles ahead. I
looked hard for some time and then said to the crew, "That's going
to be our camp tonight. We'll let our horses graze until their bellies
are full, give them a drink at the river, and maybe they can go into
a big corral. If we can do that, boy, will we ever sleep in peace."

When the horse outfit was about a mile from the ranch head-quarters, I rode ahead to make arrangements. But when I got there, I found that no one was home.

I rode back to the boys and said, "There is a great set of corrals—plenty of room in the big pen for three hundred head of stock. They have small pens, too, with stock chutes and squeezes. A real set-up for a horse breaker. What do you fellows think about setting up our camp near their yard and corralling the horses? We can have supper before dark tonight." I smiled. "I think this is my old friend's layout, but who can be sure? If they come home and let us know we're not welcome, we can soon load up and go a few miles farther. At least we won't have to hunt for our horses."

We corralled the horses in the pens and set up camp nearby. Supper was over early for a change, and the crew was happy. Little Bill played his guitar and sang some cowboy songs. Big George was clowning around and dancing on the hard-packed ground, wishing he had a bottle of hooch.

About ten o'clock that night, the ranch foreman came home. He was the old rodeo man that I was looking for. I hadn't seen him for years, but when I told him my name, we shook hands and talked. The ranchman asked a lot of questions and inquired where we were bound with the herd.

Then Cowboy George said, "Curly, we'll turn those horses out into a small pasture, a two-section field. There are no other horses out there to get mixed up with. They can graze and rest. When you want to leave, they'll be ready to travel."

Rawhide asked the foreman, "Will you be using the horse corral in the morning? If I would not be a bother to anyone, I would like to start a new saddle horse. Could I use the big corral for a while?"

"Hop right to it, cowboy," replied Cowboy George. "There are chutes, squeezes, and plenty of room for a good ride."

That night, Rawhide and I decided we would start two green horses. We arranged to get up early and go to work on them. We were hoping to add at least one more rough horse to our string of saddle stock. After dinner, we would leave and follow the river valley west.

On Monday morning, shortly after sunrise, we corralled a few horses so we could pick out some saddle-type stock. After breakfast, the excitement began. That forenoon, no work got done on the ranch. The boss and his ranch hands had perched themselves on top of a plank to watch the show.

Rawhide had a small wild bay gelding that weighed about 950 pounds and resembled a thoroughbred. His eyes were large, and he was very nervous. He was so squirmy in the chute that Rawhide had a hard job saddling him.

"What are you naming that horse?" I asked Rawhide.

The young cowboy said, "I'll tell you about sundown tonight. If he's nice with me, I'll give him a pet name. If he isn't nice, he'll get a rough name. I sure hope he behaves himself."

I had my rope on a flea-bitten, grey gelding that was real snuffy. I had handled him some, but had not had time to finish the job before leaving. He didn't act very friendly now. After a few rounds with the horse on a rope, I got him into a saddling chute and commenced to slicker him out with my saddle blanket.

Rawhide shouted, "What are you calling that little grey you're playing with? I bet it's a nice peaceful handle, isn't it?"

I answered, "Don't you remember this grey horse? This is the one I christened the Flying Dutchman the day before we left home. I think he'll be a good second to the pinto that Whalebone liked so much. He's hard to get acquainted with. Maybe he just doesn't want to be my friend too quick."

Rawhide chuckled and said, "You'll get acquainted soon enough. Just ride him out of that gate and in fifteen seconds, you'll know him."

I finished saddling and called, "Okay, boys, I'm coming out. Pick me a soft spot to fall on, just in case."

I climbed aboard, and Whalebone opened the gate. The little grey lived up to his name. Whalebone loped his horse close beside us and tried to discourage his pitching by persuading him to run.

The ranch hands on the fence were shouting, "Ride him, cowboy. Stay with him, Curly!" With this kind of encouragement, I was still on top when the grey horse came up for air.

Whalebone was shouting, "I knew you could do it, you old rang-a-tang! I'm going to enter you in the bucking contest in Compeer if we get there in time."

Big George was still asleep when he heard a big commotion around the stock corrals nearby. He rolled out of the tent to take a peek and saw dust rising, with a grey horse amidst it and me on top. He wondered if he was still dreaming. Aloud, he said, "If Curly kills himself on this trip, we'll never get any place. He better leave that kind of horse alone. Peddle him off, trade him to the Indians. If this country is as hard up as it seems to be, we may have to eat some horse meat ourselves."

He thought to himself, How nice it would be to have a gallon crock of something good this morning. Maybe alcohol. We could mix that with this river water to kill the wigglers. It would be good for snake bite, too. I'll tell Curly I need it bad.

I was working hard, trying to whirl the grey horse to the left and then to the right, so he would stop pitching. Soon, I was walking him around the big corral, letting him go as he pleased.

Then I heard Rawhide shout, "Curly, come and help me. My horse is down in the chute, and I'm afraid he'll break a leg."

By the time I got to the chute gate, the little bay horse had gotten to his feet again and was trembling like a wild deer. Rawhide was excited over the fracas. He shouted, "Curly, that saddle was hooked under the gate. It had so much pressure against it that I couldn't open the gate to let him out. I hope he'll behave and be a little more reasonable after all this excitement. He could have easily broken his neck the way he was floundering to get up."

I examined the little bay in the chute. I explained to Rawhide that only one green horse at a time can be used on the trail because they give us so much trouble for a few days. It takes extra care to look after the rider and handle the bunch of horses, too.

"Which horse do we ride away with this afternoon, the Flying Dutchman or the little bay?" I asked him.

Rawhide took a coin from his pocket. "Do you want heads or tails? Heads rides the bay and tails the grey."

He flipped the coin high in the air, and Little Bill walked over and picked it up. "Heads," he announced. "That's you, Rawhide."

The fellows sitting on the fence were chuckling amongst themselves. They were amused with the Flying Dutchman and me. A couple of these lads were in their teens and were anxious to become real cowboys. They longed for the chance to go on a drive like the one Rawhide and Little Bill were on, and they were anxious to know how Rawhide would fare with his bay horse when they were turned out of the chute into the big corral.

"Did you pick yourself a soft spot to land?" they joked.

"You can lay a big tarp about halfway across this corral. If I don't come down by then, I'll ride him across these river flats. Would you boys like to try your luck on one? We have a couple somewhere in the herd just about your size," replied Rawhide.

One of the boys answered, "I wouldn't mind trying one, but I wouldn't care to try that flying grey. He's a rodeo horse."

Rawhide climbed up on the side of the chute and looked all around. Once more, the little bay horse began to snort, stamp, and squirm. The cowboy was straddling the chute, trying to get a seat in the saddle.

Whalebone began to lecture like a college professor, "Watch your legs in that chute. Be sure to measure your buck shank so the horse doesn't jerk you overboard. When he throws his head down, get a firm hold on your rope. Keep your eyes on his head and be sure to watch every move he makes."

Rawhide smiled and said, "I've been bounced onto the ground many times before just because I was never properly instructed. When I went to school, I had to ride ten miles and I rode a fresh horse nearly every week. I can tell you, I'm no rodeo rider. My dad calls me a crazy rough-rider. Whoopee, get your horse ready, Whalebone, and keep this little fellow from jumping through the cracks between the planks."

When the gate opened, horse and rider came out. Dust flew so high they could scarcely be seen by the lads on the fence.

"Pick up your slack, cowboy," shouted Whalebone. "Lean back a little more."

Rawhide and his horse crossed the big corral fast. Whalebone

Eddy (Rawhide) Torrance, 1943. *Courtesy Marlene Davidson*

turned him from the fence and back they came. That little bay whirled, pitched, and squealed. Finally, he lost his balance and fell. Rawhide rolled and bounced away, unhurt. The horse scrambled to his feet again and bucked and squealed some more. Finally, Whalebone caught his rope and snubbed him to his saddle horn.

Rawhide was grinning, and the boys on the fence were shouting and singing their praise for him. In their mind, Rawhide was a hero. One of the boys said, "Rawhide, I sure wish I had the guts you have. I'd ride the rodeos all over the world."

I walked over to Rawhide and turned to face the youngsters on the fence. "Gentlemen, you have now seen the great Rawhide in action. You've seen his toughness, the way he bounced like a rubber ball when that horse went down. His proper name is Edward. His girlfriend calls him Eddy. The cowboys call him Rawhide."

The boys dropped down off the fence, picked up Rawhide, and carried him around the corral. Whalebone cussed the little bronco and called Rawhide to come and pile on again before the horse got his second wind. Before dinner was ready, Rawhide had ridden the little bay horse in the corral for more than an hour. He was turning each way at Rawhide's command. I was trying to do the same with the grey.

What a terrible shame it is to have to turn this horse back into the herd, I thought. I should give him a good ride for half a day at least. I guess it can't be helped. He'll have no trail today. When we leave these corrals, we have gates to go through and twelve miles across this pasture. If other horses run into our herd, we three riders would be better off on foot than to have two of us mounted on green horses. So, my nice Flying Dutchman, out you go until another time.

After dinner was over and everything packed for the next move, Whalebone inquired, "Which direction do we go from here, Curly? This place sure reminds me of the Missouri River valley. Nothing square with the world. I wouldn't even believe a compass if I was lost."

"Don't you lose that chuck wagon. You better follow the horse herd for a little way until you get your bearings," I told him.

Big George was folding a blanket across his wagon seat. He declared, "When the outfit reaches Empress, I'm gonna get myself a gallon crock."

One of the boys from the ranch asked, "What would you do with a crock if you had one?"

"Well," answered Big George, "I would leave the fellows enough to keep them happy today, I would drink some myself, and I'd rub a little on my backside. This old seat is putting corns on my rear end. By the time we reach northern British Columbia, I'll have a flat behind."

Big George and Whalebone shook hands with the ranch crew, bid them goodbye, and started their wagons northwest up the big river valley of the South Saskatchewan. Little Bill and I left Rawhide at the ranch with his new horse while we gathered the herd together from the hills and valleys of the two-section field.

When Rawhide mounted his horse, he nearly put on a repeat performance, except this time the bay stayed on all four feet. Rawhide thought things were going fairly well when the boys came back with the horse herd. But when I came to open the corral gate and haze him outside, that little bronco took one look at the open gate and all that open prairie and shot out like he was jet-propelled. He ran, bucked, and squealed. I galloped close beside Rawhide and his horse to stop them. Inside a second or two, the bay took off again as fast as he could run and buck. He went through the herd of horses that Little Bill was trying to hold together, scattering them in every direction. I soon got a hold of him and stopped his performance.

While Rawhide got his wind back, the horse was turned loose again. He ducked his head once more and bucked and groaned as if he were being killed.

Rawhide whispered to me, "That devil is about all the horse I can handle. I'm all skinned to hell now, and we haven't even left the ranch."

That same evening, Rawhide was riding his bay bronco up on the lead of the herd, all alone. When gates had to be opened, Rawhide would get down and open them. Little Bill and I were always there to see that he got mounted again. This new horse put on some kind of a show each time he was mounted, but it didn't last very long. And this time, Little Bill and I were the only audience.

North from
the Red Deer
River

THE HORSE OUTFIT TRAILED ACROSS RANCH AFTER RANCH.
When they camped in the evening, the boys went out with their
rifles, hunting for rattlers. Whalebone took his German Luger six-
shooter and practised his aim on any snakes he found.

I wrote a letter to my wife and little daughter, intending to post
it the first time we came close to a town, likely Empress, if not before.

"It won't be long now until we hear from home," I told the boys.
"Our first address was to be Compeer, Alberta, right along the
meridian between Alberta and Saskatchewan. If my wife is nearly
as lonesome as I am, there should be plenty of mail for me."

Rawhide chirped, "When you talk that way, it makes me homesick, too. I guess we better all get busy and write some letters so
they'll know we didn't drown trying to swim the Saskatchewan."

"Our horses will soon have to be checked again for brands.
That's another ten cents a head. Alberta is sure to want that much
from us. We better hold up at Empress if we can find a good place
to camp and have the RCMP come out and look at our brands once
more," I said.

When the outfit reached Empress, the boys had trouble getting
the horses past a large potato patch beside the Red Deer River. The

trail was just wide enough for wagon gear. On each side of the trail there was a fence, but most of it was down flat on the ground. The fence contained four or five strands of barbed wire and between every couple of posts, it was flat. The potato patch was irrigated property—getting the horses through without them trampling the potato patch or being cut up in the tangled wire required as much skill as loading the herd on the ferry.

The owner of the irrigated potato patch was an old gentleman by the name of Messengale. He was sitting on a sorrel horse, admiring his potato crop when the horse herd came along. He seemed pleased to see some riders from far away and asked more questions than I could answer. The old gentleman was well acquainted with the old-timers in the Val Marie district. This man had located several of the early-day ranches in southwestern Saskatchewan, shortly after the turn of the century, such as the 76 ranch along the Saskatchewan River. He had helped build up their first camps and had planted the first trees around the yard. The crew remembered passing this ranch; they had seen the huge cottonwood trees, as well as their irrigation system. The large green meadows stood out on the prairie like an oasis in a desert.

A bridge of tremendous size spanned the Red Deer River near its junction with the Saskatchewan. Empress was located at the point between the two large streams.

"I'll show you a good place if you want to set up camp and a real good place to hold your horses," Mr. Messengale said. "Take everything across the bridge and have a look. The Red Deer River will be on the north, so your horses won't drift that way, and part of the south side has a fence."

This fellow had been a ranchman all his life. He had trailed horses all over Alberta and Saskatchewan in the early days, selling them to the settlers, and he had travelled many parts of the Peace River country on horseback with pack outfits. Hardly a place in the west could be mentioned that he had not been or knew something about. He said that he had been in western Canada and western USA since 1885. For all of his age, he still looked about as tough as an old Missouri mule.

Mr. Messengale and I rode across the bridge, side by side, behind the herd, and I listened while the old gent kept up a continual conversation.

"How old do you take me for?" he asked.

"It's hard for me to guess. You still sit in a saddle far straighter than many young men, and you're still riding a good horse."

The old man chuckled and said, "I'm eighty-five." Then he asked, "Are you any judge of a horse's age, Curly? Could you tell me how old my pony might be?"

I took a peek at the sorrel horse's head and could see grey in the hair around its eyes.

"That's a good horse you're riding, Mister. He seems to know his stuff around a bunch of horses, too. I can tell he's no colt, but, of course, I could guess wrong by ten years without looking at his teeth."

The old fellow chuckled. "My horse is twenty-eight years old. I broke him to ride myself and owned him since he was a three-year-old."

"Where can I find the RCMP office?" I inquired. "I have to have the horses' brands inspected for the province of Alberta."

The old gent replied, "I'll show you. I know the police officer real well. He's a great guy, too. He's an old-timer himself and will be glad to meet you, Curly."

When I was introduced to the Mountie, I was introduced as an old friend. Mr. Messengale said, "Why sure, Pete, he knows all my old friends. He even knew a lot of the old boys who have died since I've been back there. He's taking his horses away from the drought area, trying to find feed for them. Curly has a good idea of what he's up against."

The old fellow chuckled from way down deep in his throat and said, "Pete, Curly and his crew are staying over for a day and I intend to show them around this town. Don't pick us up if we make a little extra noise."

After Mr. Messengale and I visited with the Mountie for about half an hour, the officer told me, "I'm leaving town this afternoon and do not have time to inspect all of those horses. It would take me at least one whole day. If your outfit is travelling north from here, it would not be so important anyhow. Follow the meridian line, and if a cop bothers you from the Alberta side, just push the herd across the line into Saskatchewan. If police on that side make any trouble, just drive the herd back again. You may not be bothered much for another week. The fellow that will bother you will have far more time than I have at present."

The Mountie wished us well and told us about thousands of acres of wild hay in the Slave Lake district, where he was once stationed. He also talked about the old Peace River Drag, the only trail going through that wilderness of brush and poplar.

In the meantime, Big George was having the time of his life. He had met new friends in Empress and was enjoying the break from the trail. Some of the other lads in the crew figured he must have gotten the crock he had been talking about.

"I wonder how much will be left for rubbing on his backside?" Little Bill asked. "Maybe he'll just rub the bottle on it and try to cure his complaint from the inside. He talks a lot about snake bite. Do you suppose he'll save a little bit for the road?"

Little Bill and Rawhide planned to go out dancing for a couple of hours that evening, as they had met some nice ladies about their age. The old gent had done them grand.

I intended to keep an eye on the horses and the camp. I looked at my map of Saskatchewan that showed the townships and ranges. Early in life, I had learned all about the section lines. Now, I was counting the townships and figuring the distance north to the Sounding Lake country, situated in Alberta, not far west of the meridian line that I intended to follow.

The next morning, I said to the crew, "It's six miles across a township. We can go north here for a hundred miles, then we'll cross about five railroad tracks and come close to three small towns. This map doesn't show one dang creek in a hundred miles. A fellow told me this morning that the thermometer read ninety-eight at eight o'clock. Whalebone, make sure the water barrel and cans are full before you leave the Red Deer River. Hot water will keep us from choking to death until we can find a spring or a good well. A good rain would look like a million dollars. What do you think, Whalebone?"

Whalebone was smiling. He had been teasing the boys about skylarking all night at the dance and was enjoying his own jokes when he heard me mention rain. "It sure don't look much like rain this morning. We're not much used to rain anyhow. Don't begin the day worrying about water. The horses have a whole river full to start. Who knows? We may find plenty before night."

The boys wrote some letters, and we mailed them from Empress. They told their folks how much they were enjoying their trip with the horses and of their new experiences. They felt sure they were toughening up with the daily exercise of riding and Whalebone's bait. They told about the fine way they were treated at Empress and of the good time they had had at the dance, as well as the way they spent their evenings on the trail, with music and song. They gave a fair picture of how we loaded the ferry and praised me for getting the herd safely across the Saskatchewan River.

Late that day, and after about forty miles of hard riding, we halted beside a small, slowly seeping spring. The horses drank and splashed in the mud. The sun sank low, as usual, and the air cooled off for the night. It was a satisfied crew that slept under the stars that night.

Friends
along the Trail

ONE DAY, ABOUT NOON, THE CHUCK WAGON STOPPED beside a small clear lake, south of Compeer.

"I'm going to stop here for a week and just lay in the water," exclaimed Whalebone. "There's lots of grass here for the stock. You fellows won't have much night herding to do, so you can take a turn at the frying pan. These young fellows are getting kind of runty on my biscuits, anyhow."

We set up camp beside some bushes that were close to the lake shore and turned the wagon horses into the herd to graze and roll in the fine grass. I caught a fresh saddle horse from the herd and tied him to the wheel of Big George's wagon.

"Right after dinner, I'm going into Compeer to get a bag full of mail for you fellows. It's only four or five miles to town. Is there anything else you waddies want me to bring back this afternoon?" I asked.

Rawhide shouted, "You can't call us fellows cowpokes or waddies. We're the mustang wranglers. When you go to town, you can bring back some gum and cigarettes for me."

Big George replied, "How about a case of beer, Curly? Will that pony pack a case of beer without spilling you? I'm awfully tired of this river water."

Whalebone remarked, "I'm short of chewing tobacco, snuff, and a few odds and ends for the wagon. You better take a couple of sacks with you, Curly, to carry it all back. Be sure you come back today."

I returned with the mail, and each of the boys had two or more letters. They all seemed very happy, except for Whalebone. He put his letters in his pocket and did not read any of them. The rest of the crew reread their letters several times. My wife and little daughter had so much to tell. She said that the country was still very dry, and the topsoil continued to blow. The potato patches had dried up, and the small potatoes would be all used before digging time.

That evening, several town folks gathered at the lake to swim and enjoy the evening breeze and pure prairie air. Some came with teams, while a few others had cars. They all enjoyed a party around the chuck wagon.

Little Bill strummed his guitar and sang cowboy songs for the young folks as they gathered around. He played "Turkey in the Straw," while Rawhide and Big George began to clog-dance in the sand by the lake shore. The crowd was whooping it up. Someone found a few bottles of beer for Big George, and he was in a fair way to entertain. Little Bill called for me to get my lariat rope and do some rope stunts. Most of his smiles were directed at a very pretty little girl of sixteen or seventeen years with light golden hair. All were in the mood for fun. It was not often that the lads had a chance to entertain the prairie girls. In the bush country, their fun would be lacking.

Someone brought a lariat rope to me and said, "Hop to it. Show us what you can do. Make a big loop and jump in and out. Let's go!"

I took the rope, straightened out the kinks, and started a loop spinning. Then, I walked around the camp in the centre of the spinning loop.

Little Bill slipped away and came back leading his pet horse. He saddled her carefully, brushing her so she would shine. He mounted her and rode slowly away from camp, out along the shore of the lake. Everyone watched. When he had gone about twenty rods away, he turned the roan back toward camp. He rose out of the saddle, stood up on the mare, and gently galloped back.

With trick roping and trick riding, music and song, the small crowd spent a grand evening. Little Bill persuaded the girl with the golden hair to return with her friends the next day. The young riders were happy when they rolled into their blankets about midnight.

About noon the following day, while the riders were out looking after the horses, Whalebone began to prepare dinner for the crew. I came back to camp earlier than the rest and found the cook alone.

"What's the matter, Whalebone? You seem so sad. I hope you didn't get any bad news yesterday. What's eating you anyhow?" I asked.

"Listen to me a minute, Curly, while we're alone. Do you know that I never went to school in my life. I never learned to read a damn thing. Can I depend entirely on you?"

Whalebone stirred something in a kettle on the stove for a minute then whispered slowly, "That little girl I left back home on the prairie, to wait for me, is a school teacher. Next spring, when the grass starts to green up, we're going on our honeymoon."

The young riders did not come back to camp for their dinner until one o'clock. Before they returned, Whalebone took both letters from his pocket.

"See what they say, Curly, before the boys get in for dinner."

I looked at the date stamp on the letters and said, "This one is nearly two weeks old. I guess we better take them in their turn. I'll write an answer to these letters for you sometime this afternoon when we're alone. You can just tell me what to write. This is a private affair, Whalebone, what do you say?"

I opened a letter, took out a small photo, and handed it to the cook.

"Is that her, cowboy?" I asked.

I read the neatly written letter. When I glanced at Whalebone, I saw a tear in his eye. He blinked once or twice, and the tear disappeared. After I had read both letters, he was in good spirits once again.

Whalebone asserted mildly, "I don't know how in the hell I'd have ever read those letters without your help."

That afternoon, when the boys left the camp to see the herd again, I had a chance to reply to Whalebone's sweetheart for him.

In about half an hour, Big George awoke from a nap in the shade.

He walked across to the wagon and asked, "Would you mind writing a letter for me?"

"It would be a pleasure."

"My only living sister is a nun at Duck Lake. I don't read too good, but I'm worse at letter writing. My French and English want to get all tangled up. Maybe you had better read this letter out loud to me. I know she's okay, but she has asked too many questions. She doesn't want me to have a bottle of beer, but I get so dang dry that my tongue gets thick. I'll be sixty-four this year. She's all I have in the family line, but she doesn't need any help from me, and I don't have too many years left to have some fun. What is an old bachelor like myself supposed to do, Curly?"

A few days later, the outfit camped in the Sounding Lake country. There were several lakes in the area, as well as some small trees and taller grass than what grew farther south. The boys noticed that the grass was more abundant, but the quality didn't compare with the short grass in the country near Val Marie. We could all see very plainly that the country was changing. Instead of open prairie, we were now travelling amidst clusters of small bush.

"We must be away from the drought area now," I said. "I've noticed better gardens and crops. A fellow told me yesterday that the land between here and Edmonton is mostly farming country. Many cattle are raised here as well. Some big dairy herds, near the towns, supply folks with milk, and they grow pigs by the thousands. We can expect plenty of trouble finding enough water for the horses in the next 150 miles. That will mean some more long days ahead in the saddle."

The town of Metiskow, Alberta, was our new address for mail. "I sure hope our letters from home get there ahead of us," I said. "If we could just find a good camping place when we get there like we had at the lake where we got our mail the first time, we could rest up again. I could use some more sleep, how about you fellows?"

Each day took the horse outfit closer to Edmonton. We were bothered, nearly every day for a week, about brand fees and inspections. We were checked several times by a man who wore a moustache. Each time, this policeman grew tougher, even nasty.

I told this fellow, "Just follow along until we find grass and water where we can hold up and you can go ahead and check. If we try to check them here, you know they would just tramp down a hundred acres of these wheat crops."

The corporal and I talked it over, while the herd trailed on ahead. We agreed to have the horses corralled in the stock yards when we reached the town of Hardisty, where the RCMP was stationed. Metiskow was situated in a bluff country setting. All hands were anxious to get their mail there, and everyone had their eyes open for a campsite. In the middle of the afternoon, the horses came to a lovely slough of water along the roadside about two miles east of Metiskow. The water was nearly two feet deep, and the green grass was growing around it about a foot and a half high. The stock rushed into the water for a drink, and when they had quenched their thirst, they began at once to eat the luscious grass on the roadway. We were cheering about this good luck, and the boys agreed to hold the herd while I went into town to pick up the mail.

Not long after I left camp to go into town, an old gentleman from a nearby farm walked out onto the trail from behind a poplar bluff. He stood on the road for a few minutes admiring the herd of horses, then walked a little nearer to the boys, who were sitting on the grass watching their ponies graze. He seemed to be a very friendly fellow.

Whalebone began to ask him questions about the road ahead. The old gent said, "Water is sure to be scarce for the next hundred miles. The Ribstone Creek is not so far from here, but it's low, too. The surrounding creek flats are hay meadows for half a mile on each side."

The old fellow asked the boys where they had come from and where they were going with the horses. Before long, he wanted to know who was in charge of the crew. Whalebone told him about me and said that I had just gone into town to pick up the mail.

The visitor repeated the name Gunter several times, then announced, "It seems very funny, but years ago, some of my best friends had that same name. Can you tell me where he was raised? I want to have a talk with him before you leave here today."

This stranger was a tall, thin man of seventy-five years. He had the largest ears the boys had ever seen. He told the crew that in his

Finding adequate grass and water for the horses was a constant concern.
Courtesy Don Shapley

younger days, he had been a lumberjack. In later years, he bought land in the Metiskow district and farmed until he retired from heavy work a few years back.

He laughed and said, "I still have to eat, so I got myself a job hauling the mail on a twenty-mile mail route with a span of mules."

The old fellow was still visiting with the boys when I returned with the mail. When he saw me, he jumped to his feet like a kid and shouted, "Is your dad's name Tom, Hank, or Frank?"

I replied, "My dad's name is Tom. How did you guess?"

"Well," he laughed, "you sure resemble some of those old boys I used to know in the lumber woods."

When the stranger found out that he knew my folks and that he had lived among my relatives when he was a small boy, he seemed very happy. He knew my parents, older brothers and sisters, uncles and aunts, and neighbours.

"If you think real hard, young feller, you may remember my second wife. She cooked in the Hamilton house."

"Good lordy, man, she was my Sunday school teacher!"

The old fellow shouted, "Turn your horses in this gate and put your roundup wagon under those trees beside the house. We'll celebrate tonight for old-times' sake."

When the large band of horses raced past the bluff by the farm house, it caused Grandma and her granddaughter to wonder a great deal. They went to the window and watched but could not understand where all the horses were coming from.

It was not long before three riders appeared. Following the riders came a roundup wagon. Grandpa was walking ahead, with Big George's dog running playfully beside him. Both wagons parked under the large trees near the side of the house. Grandpa watched closely as the wagon men unharnessed their horses and turned them into the herd.

The old fellow told Whalebone just how much better his mule team was than the best team of horses. Whalebone noticed an old grey mule standing across the yard with its ears flopping, dozing in the shade. He could not help laughing to himself, but agreed that the mule was a very tough, wise, and splendid animal for most jobs. Little Bill was smiling, too, as he noticed a young lady at the house watching through the window.

The old gentleman said, "Hurrah, Curly, come and meet my old lady. See if she remembers you. Her memory is far better than mine."

As we entered the house, my new friend said, "Ma, you will never guess, in ten years, who this kid is. Take a good look at him and name him if you can. He was in your Sunday school class at Salem Corners. Take a good look now, Ma."

I was all smiles to be among old acquaintances so unexpectedly. I grinned broadly as the old gentleman remarked, "It must be nearly twenty years since we have been at Salem Corners, and you couldn't be expected to remember all the curly-headed kids in your Sunday class."

Grandma was still staring hard. "Richard, why don't you tell me who he is? I used to teach thirty children in a class back in those days."

When Grandpa told her whose son I was, she groaned, heaved herself to her feet, and kissed me. She whispered, "The good Lord has brought you here for a purpose. I haven't seen anyone from that part of the world since I was a young woman. Meet my grand-daughter, Clara. She lives north of town, but she's looking after us codgers today and tomorrow."

The farmer's wife was somewhere in her late seventies. Her health was not as good as it used to be, and arthritis seemed to have a clamp on her knees. She was hardly able to care for a house and a husband. She tried her best to keep their home together and did not complain. The old gent had a son who was farming in the district, and their granddaughter often came to help out her grandparents.

For the next hour, the old folks asked questions, and I tried to answer them the best I could.

"Both my parents are still living and are fairly well," I told them. "They pioneered in southwestern Saskatchewan about twenty years ago, when the country was thrown open to the homesteaders. Just a few years ago, the railroad was built and Val Marie became our town. That shortened the long trails to Ponteix and Cadillac for us. For three years, we've had drought in that corner, and now we have a bad depression riding high. My oldest brother, Seth, has a homestead in the Peace River country and my sister Eva is living out there, too. That's where we're heading now."

Tears were building in Grandma's eyes as she exclaimed, "What a terrible long trip on horseback. It must be awful looking after all those horses night and day. You won't get to your brother's before Christmas."

At suppertime, the old fellow brought a jug of choke-cherry wine to the wagon and poured nearly a cupful for each of the boys. He chuckled a little and remarked, "This will be a starter. When you fellows get into town tonight, kick up your heels for me, too. I'm slipping some the last few years."

"Maybe some of the boys might go into Metiskow tonight," I told him, "but I'm staying here to visit as much as I can with you and Grandma. This is a treat I never expected. Our horses are inside a fence, and the gate is closed. We'll all enjoy a real sleep tonight."

Some People
Think a Range Rider
Has No Feelings

....

A LARGE BLACK CLOUD WAS HOVERING IN THE WESTERN sky as we watered the horses at Ribstone Creek. The outfit passed part of the Wainright Buffalo Park, where fences were very high and sturdy. The shaggy old buffalo chewing grass beside the road spooked the horses. They did not like the smell, look, or actions of those monarchs of the plains. They snorted and raised their heads high, ready to take off if a buffalo chanced to come their way.

Rawhide and Little Bill had never seen a buffalo before and were very interested in this bunch of about seven head. They were remembering their history lessons from school, about the wholesale slaughter of these animals. They were also thinking of the guts the Indians must have had, in earlier times, to attack such a ferocious beast with a bareback horse, armed with nothing more than a bow and arrow.

Little Bill said, "It's doubtful a small calibre rifle would pierce their hair and thick hide. An arrow to one of those huge animals would be like a sliver in my finger."

The large cloud overhead kept spreading and getting darker.

"Boys, it looks like we are in for a good rain," I said. "The air feels so different this afternoon. Our tent hasn't had much of a chance to turn away any water so far. The first place we see some grass, we better hole up like these pocket gophers we're seeing. We better get our slickers from the chuck wagon, too."

Rawhide exclaimed, "Why, Curly, that cayuse of mine would die of heart failure if I tried to ride him in a slicker. How about yours? Could you mount him with a slicker flapping?"

"Some of our green-broken horses are hard enough to mount without anything flapping in the wind," I answered, "but if we're caught in a rainstorm, mine will have to get used to it. Mud, rain, or wind, a slicker and a bucking horse are a cowboy's life."

We found some grass and made camp early in the day. The cloud grew until it covered all of the western sky. Thunder rolled and echoed back and forth, and a few drops of rain fell as a warning.

The lads pounded tent pegs while Big George rustled up some dry wood for the cook. The air became so heavy that Whalebone's stove did not want to draw. It sputtered and coughed, and the smoke stayed near the ground.

Whalebone cussed and chewed tobacco with a vengeance. "Roll around here you rang-a-tangs and get a pile of dry wood for tomorrow," he demanded. "Get it under the tarp. Hell is going to break loose here pretty soon, and my dang stove won't draw enough to melt butter. I have to bake an ovenful of biscuits, or you guys will have no supper tonight."

The boys set up the tent under a spreading, big-branched tree and pegged it solid. The beds were placed inside the tent.

Whalebone cussed the boys for cutting green wood and sent them back for a supply of dry. He was scolding like an old hen with her chicks. "You prairie boys may know something about picking prairie chips, but you're not on the prairie any longer. You'll likely learn a whole lot about cutting wood before we get all the way across Alberta's green forests. We may have to hew our trail part way."

Both boys were laughing and thinking that Whalebone's school marm must have sent his ring back or worse. Meanwhile, Whalebone was having terrible trouble with his stove. It refused to bake his biscuits, and the smoke belched out where the draught should have been taking in fresh air.

Whalebone continued shouting, "I'll never get supper this way. I'm getting my eyes and lungs smoked out. I'm going to try two or three more lengths of stove pipe. You dang loafers, get busy. Climb up in that wagon and get some more pipes for this thing! They must be under the big tarp, or maybe they're in Big George's wagon. Get a move on. Roll your spurs for once. This is only a mosquito smudge. You fellows think you have troubles trying to look after a few horses, you should just try cooking for a change."

Rawhide answered, "You crotchety old cook, there isn't a stove pipe within a hundred miles of us. When you let those ponies run away with the chuck wagon, we lost everything that was loose."

Whalebone shouted, "Hell's bells! No supper tonight, and we may all drown before morning by the look of the sky."

"It's going to be a nasty job for an inspector to inspect the herd's brands if it keeps raining," I said. "The stock yards will be a mud hole a foot deep. When the RCMP at Hardisty inspects our stock tomorrow, we must demand a written trail permit so we won't have any more trouble while crossing Alberta. Just yesterday, my Pigeon mare spooked at that cop's car, slipped in the mud, and fell flat on my legs. That contrary cuss laughed like it was a joke. Some people think a range rider has no feelings. I dang near broke my leg. Every time they turn their car crosswise on the trail, we have trouble!"

The rain poured down all night, and puddles of water spread on the flat ground. The wind blew a tree branch against the top of the tent, causing a bad tear. There was a continual drip from near the top. The bed rolls were settled into the mud, and everything was well soaked. The water had nowhere to run on this flat ground, and so much rain fell that the ground could not soak it up. Everyone thought about home and the comforts of all other trades.

The next morning, breakfast was a cold bite of what could be found in the cupboard. About ten o'clock, I left the soaked camp and rode into Hardisty to make arrangements for a brand inspection. The rain had not let up in the least. I was already soaking wet but wore a pair of heavy Angora chaps with my slicker on top as my horse sloshed through mud and water in the steady downpour. I reached town and found the RCMP office at about eleven o'clock. The corporal was at home, hoping that no one would call him out on a wet day like this, when I rapped on his door.

Small streams of water ran off my chaps and slicker as I stood just inside the door of the office and stated my business. The inspector promised to examine the brands when the herd reached Hardisty.

"Can you make some arrangements for us to use the stock yards here in town?" I asked. "We're camped a few miles east and will be along about two o'clock."

When I returned to camp, I found that Whalebone had placed his stove inside the tent and was trying his best to get a hot dinner for the crew.

At two o'clock that afternoon, the horses were all corralled in the stock yards along the railroad tracks in Hardisty. The inspector arrived soon after in his slicker and rubber boots to look at the brands. He was well prepared for this nasty job, as he was wearing an oil-skin hood on his slicker.

Before he finished, he had mud in his eyes and hair, and his slicker looked as if he had found it in a badger hole. The horses kept milling around in the corral, splashing mud over their backs. The inspector looked at one horse, and before he could find a brand, it would disappear behind the others. He went farther into the corral for a look, but only for a minute, before he was obliged to crawl up on the fence for safety. This man did not care too much for his job this day. He wiped mud from his eyes and made many peculiar faces.

"Someone should have done this job a hundred miles back," he complained.

This business had been going on for about twenty minutes when a long freight train pulled in beside the stock yards. The wheels of the old steam locomotive clanked. Steam hissed, the engine roared, and the ground seemed to vibrate. The penned horses stood nearly two deep from fright.

While the inspector was having trouble with the horses, the riders watched the train. Many empty box cars and flat cars were westward bound, with men sitting side by side, their feet hanging over the edges. It looked as if they were sitting on a very large bench. From the top of the box cars, men were waving their hands at the crew. The freight riders had no coats, no food, no shelter. The train hustled them along across Alberta in the rainstorm.

Little Bill was deep in thought. He told the rest of the boys, "I sure felt bad last night when the tent was leaking, but we're not so bad off. We can get under a tree, or perhaps into some farmer's shed or barn, but those poor guys up on that flat car just hump themselves up like a bronc, while water runs down their neck continually."

Through the big country—where water was supposed to be scarce—we found water in abundance. It must have been the rainy season as it poured nearly every day. The wagon wheels rolled the mud around themselves until they resembled steel-wheeled tractors. Each wagon was pulled by four horses, and they were all slipping and sliding for several days. The herd was able to get plenty of water from the ditches. It was tough going, but what the boys disliked the most was setting up their tent in the rain and having mud for a wrangler's bed.

High Adventure
and a New Passenger

THE CROPS IN THIS PART OF ALBERTA LOOKED WONDER-fully good. Oats, wheat, and barley grew as high as the fence, thick and heavy. Grass grew in abundance along the roadside, and there was water in every pothole. The horses were getting plenty to eat, and I aimed to see that they always had a full belly.

Big George had been quiet lately. He was not exactly enjoying this wet spell of weather. He tried to keep himself as dry as possible so he would not get sick. Lately, he had been wearing his heavy coonskin overcoat.

As he admired the crops along the road, Big George remarked to the crew, "It's too dang bad that a farmer can't get the cost of production for the food he produces: wheat, oats, barley, milk, eggs, butter, meat, and vegetables. I think it's far worse here, where they have bumper crops of everything. I don't suppose I could get twenty-five dollars for my best horse, and everyone knows that plenty of work horses are needed in a farming district like this. Nothing seems to have any value."

He gave his black dog a friendly rub on the ears and spoke to him in French for a minute or two, just as if the dog knew exactly what it was all about.

The rain let up for a couple of days, but the road was still slippery and muddy. We were travelling northwest, trying to direct our course toward Fort Saskatchewan. The soil through this section of the country was almost black and very productive. Days were long and campsites were far apart.

For several days, we could see something shining in the distance. After inquiring, we were told it was a large water tank at the penitentiary in Fort Saskatchewan. This bright tank, shining in the sun, became our guide.

Fort Saskatchewan was another address where we would pick up our mail. All hands were anxious to reach this good town, and we were hoping that when we got to the river, we would find an ideal crossing.

We found a camping spot with plenty of grass and a slough full of water. This large tract of idle land was once owned by some big company and was being held for speculation. Most of the road allowances were fenced, and there were hundreds of acres of unfenced grass. This saved us many hours of night herding.

Everything was packed for another day of hard riding when Rawhide galloped suddenly into camp and exclaimed, "Curly, that big black Flying U mare with the white strip on her face is having a colt. What will we do with her? And with a baby colt? Can we move her?"

"You'd better take my Luger and do away with it. It won't be able to travel for weeks," said Whalebone. "Our early colts are showing bad effects from the trail already, and we're not even halfway there."

"Don't do that, cowboy," I called out. "We'll stay here another day for the old mare's sake. Then we'll unpack a couple of feet in the back end of Big George's wagon and carry the little fellow in there. It will mean more chores for us, but I can't kill the innocent little thing. After a week or two on the trail, we'll all love that little colt."

The newborn was a shiny, chubby, black filly. She had a white strip down her face from her ears to her nose. We watched as she wobbled to her feet and staggered about until she nuzzled the wild Flying U mare.

The mare was a good mother. She was about nine years old and had always lived on the range in a wild state like the antelope. She had never been halter-broken. The only time man had placed a hand upon her was when she was branded at the Flying U ranch, near Val Marie. She had already raised several colts, and most of them had grown to a good size for farm work. She had an udder like a cow's, and it looked as if this little colt would get plenty of rich milk.

She didn't want the boys to get too close to her new offspring, though. She would whinny and dash madly away, hoping her colt would follow. When she returned to her colt, her ears would lay flat, warning us to beware.

After Little Bill had handled the little colt for a week, loading and unloading it, he began to think of the fun he could have with it. "This colt will think that we're her mother. I suppose we'll have to rope her each time we want to load her. If she follows that old black mare when she's able to run, we'll need our fastest horse in order to catch her."

Rawhide and I went into the herd to check the horses and colts. "All of our colts have swollen ankles," I announced, "as well as some of our yearlings. The swelling is caused from hard travelling and hard ground. Colts and yearlings never stand the hard road like the older horses. I guess it's because their bones are softer and their tendons are weaker. Still, we could not take the mares and leave their colts. They'll get over it in time, if they don't cripple up while we're on the trail. We'll have to favour them some and take it easy."

Since the outfit was staying over another day, the two young cowboys were wondering what they could do to amuse themselves.

"I'm going to ride around and put up any gates that may be down and see that these fences are all in good enough shape," decided Rawhide. "Then I'm going to sleep until suppertime. The stock have plenty to keep them happy without me watching."

When Little Bill and Rawhide rode back to camp for their dinner, we had a visitor. A dairy farmer who lived in the neighbourhood brought an armful of fresh rhubarb, a gallon of milk, and some vegetables. He had seen the crew setting up camp the night before, and since we were still here, he wondered if we could give him a hand with something.

The stranger was a middle-aged man. He introduced himself to the lads and asked, "Are there any cowboys among the crew? I'm looking for a man that has nerve enough to put a ring in my bull's nose. I can't do it alone. He's a three-year-old shorthorn. Lately, he's been getting dangerous to have around, and I have a growing family to watch out for. Maybe if he had a ring in his nose, it might help some."

Whalebone shouted, "How about you, Curly? You and I can milk wild cows on foot. Why can't we ring his bull?"

"Sure, Mister," I replied. "We'll fix him for you."

The stranger pointed his finger to the west and said, "That's my silo that you can see a couple of miles away. I'll look for you sometime this afternoon." The farmer drove back to his home behind the bluff, wearing a smile.

After dinner, Rawhide asked, "What horses do you fellows want for your job today?"

I replied, "Bring in old Captain for me. Which one do you want, Whalebone?"

"I guess Nightmare will be okay. Something that can move fast enough to get out of the way in a pinch."

The two ponies were brought to camp and tied to the wagon wheel, where we saddled them. When I finished, I strolled over to the cupboard in the chuck wagon and found a whetstone, then walked back to my horse, sharpening the small blade on my jackknife.

"What in the world are you going to do with that knife?" Whalebone asked. "We're only supposed to put a ring in his nose."

"You know, those bull rings are supposed to be self-piercing, and the tissue that we have to pierce is very thin, but it can sure be tough on an old bull. When I pull his nose out a ways, I'll run this small blade through first. The ring can then be put through and connected quickly. Which end of the bull do you want to take, Whalebone?"

"It's a big job for me to heel an animal, so I better take the front end. You can snag his back leg, and we'll stretch him out. It's no use taking chances with an ugly bull."

When we rode around the bluff that afternoon, we saw a dairy herd, a good set of barns, a high silo, and a fairly large yard. There was a fence made from peeled poles, about four poles high. Inside this pen was the shorthorn bull. When he saw us coming his way, he began to paw the ground and commenced to bellow. He curved his back into a hump and threw sand onto it with his foot, using it like a shovel.

The farmer's wife and five children came out to meet us. She begged her husband to be careful. "That brute might hurt some-one," she worried. "It would be much better to build something to hold the bull's head secure than to take any chances."

"Just give us five minutes and Curly will have that ring in the bull's nose for keeps," Whalebone reassured her.

We rode into the low pen together, our lariat ropes in hand. The bull bounded halfway across the corral and stopped short.

"He has a good mind to attack us," I said. "I'd hate to be on foot in here."

Whalebone's rope shot out and snared the bull by his thick neck. The bull hopped around like an acrobat, ready for battle. I flipped a loop on his hind leg, and our two horses stretched the ornery animal out as far as he could go. The bull bellowed with rage. He stood on three feet for a few seconds and then flopped over onto his side and lay still. I left Captain to hold on alone while I hopped off my saddle and started to work with my knife. In almost no time, the ring was in place, and I turned the bull's nose high in the air and took off Whalebone's neck loop. Whalebone mounted my horse, and I made a dash for the fence, jumping over it in a hurry as the bull got to his feet. Whalebone flipped the rope slack on the bull's leg, and when it came off, he rode out through the gate, leading his own pony.

The whole family had been watching. "Boys," said the farmer, "that was teamwork. Do you fellows follow the shows together?"

Whalebone answered, "Mister, where we come from, this is every-day chores. We're not show men at all—just hard-working, everyday cowpokes. You should see some of our experts perform. The south country has the best cowhands in the world. The Montana boys have the know-how, too. We have two lads on our crew who we're breaking in. They'll be good before long. They can ride like a bur. The only way a horse can get rid of them is to lay down and roll. They sleep on their horses when they're night herding. Give those fellows another year and the Calgary Stampede will know about that pair. They work together, too. You should see our Rawhide go when he starts a new saddle horse. You'd think he was born in a saddle."

"So long, folks," I said. "Whalebone had better keep some of that sermon for another Sunday."

The farmer and his wife were very pleased to have this job done and thanked us for coming to their aid. We left the farm in good spirits and rode around the bluff, back to our camp.

Before evening, the clouds began to gather in a peculiar fashion. The main cloud, to the northwest, looked black, with streaks of grey. It seemed to be coming toward us at a terrific rate.

Big George looked at the sky for a minute, then exclaimed, "Holy cow, that's a wind! It looks like a cyclone. We better peg the tent a little better."

In less than half an hour, the clouds had gathered, their wispy tails trailing below. Very soon, the rain began to pelt down.

Big George put on his coonskin overcoat, and the rest of us donned slickers and dove into the tent. The rain came down by the bucketful, and a furious wind arose. The rain soon turned to hail, and the tent started to bob and weave in the wind. Everyone was huddled close together so our heads would not touch the sides of the small tent. We were hoping that the storm would pass without damaging anything.

The hail let up for a couple of minutes, and the wind switched directions. Then the hail struck again, with a vengeance. The wind and rain soaked and lashed at the tent until, finally, it could stand no longer. It jumped clear off the spot where we had been huddled and blew right over the chuck wagon. Tent pegs flew and Whale-bone cussed. Everybody ran to get under the wagon. Hailstones were bouncing twenty feet high, and the rain ran a puddle of water under the wagon in seconds.

Rawhide's pony was tied to the wagon wheel and stood with his head beneath the wagon box to get away from the hail. When the tent came flying over the wagon, it was more than his nerves could stand. He pulled so hard that he nearly tipped the wagon over before his lead rope broke and he galloped away into the storm.

The large herd of horses had found a bluff and huddled up. The wind blew hard enough to cause the chuck wagon to move. The five of us crawled along on all fours, trying to stay under it. The canvas blew off the wagon top, and everything got drenched.

"There'll be no dry wood, and our flour will be soaked!" Whalebone shouted.

The hail finally quit, and the clouds and wind moved on. We all compared bumps on our heads and hands to see who had the most hail damage.

Once again, we set up the tent in the mud. The bedding was soaked. Blankets were placed over the wagon box to dry a little before being rolled out in the mud for our beds.

The hail had caused the temperature to drop. The dampness in the air and the piles of hailstones were sure to change the weather for a day or two.

Whalebone ordered the boys to set up his stove inside the tent for the night, though the wet wood made more of a smudge than heat. Big George curled up by the stove in his big coonskin coat, his black dog cuddled close beside him. Before he went to sleep that night, he sang to the boys, "Let the rest of the world go by . . . " The rest of us were quiet, thinking of the good beds we had left behind back home.

The next morning before breakfast, Rawhide asked me, "Did you ever see a storm like that before?"

"Yes, sir," I replied. "Many times, and some far worse."

"Such as what?" Little Bill asked in surprise. "That's the worst hail pounding I've ever had. If that chuck wagon hadn't been close when the tent took off, we'd all be dead and maybe buried, too."

I began to describe some worse catastrophes. "Now, cowboy, did you ever read of floods where rivers would raise twenty feet in a few hours? If a fellow was a poor swimmer and got caught up in one, that would be worse.

"In the summer of 1912, a cyclone raged right through the city of Regina. It didn't last very long, but it plucked bricks out of walls, threw freight cars over top of each other, knocked down solid buildings made of brick, mortar, and timber, and twisted up iron bars until they looked like haywire. I'd say that was a catastrophe. We only have a bump or two on our heads."

Little Bill was listening closely, trying to imagine it all. His eyes were large, and he was staring hard.

"Curly," he said, "did all that really happen in Regina?"

"Just as true as we are camped here in this mud hole. Many people were killed, and others were hurt and homeless. My dad saw where the storm had passed through the city. Once in 1916, I saw a homesteader's house jump twenty-five feet into the air and come down headfirst, thirty rods away. That's the power of wind.

"Yesterday was a mild one, but I didn't like it, either. Lightning can clip your ear off as slick as a knife blade. In a bad lightning storm, you should get clear away from your horse. Animals seem to draw electricity. I remember a storm one evening when I was riding near some fences. My saddle horse dropped onto his knees several times from shock. I didn't expect to get home alive that time. My nerves kept spurring me, but I wasn't hurt at all."

Through this fine farming district between Czar and other points, there was some terrible hail damage. At many places along our route, we saw crops that had been hailed out one hundred percent. At other places, the storm had lifted slightly and only about fifty percent of the crops were damaged. The hailstorm had moved in the same direction we were travelling, so we saw its effects for many miles. It was sad to see so many miles of nice crops all hailed out, but people who had hail insurance were smiling.

A farmer who visited the horse camp one evening tried to explain the plight of the Alberta farmer. "The top grade for wheat this year will be under thirty cents a bushel. Oats, just a few cents. A new binder to harvest this crop is several hundred dollars. Threshing will be fifteen cents a bushel. How many granaries would a big farmer need for his oat crop? Combining is three and a half dollars per acre, and it must be swathed in this part of Alberta, or a combine will give too many green kernels. That would knock the price another six or eight cents. We're really up against it this year."

And we thought we had it rough.

Heel Flies
or High Water

THE CREW WAS GETTING FAIRLY WELL ACQUAINTED WITH the little black colt. We loaded her and unloaded her at each camping place. The Flying U mare was never far from the wagon. She would follow close behind her colt, whinnying and switching her long tail. Her colt would whinny right back but seemed very satisfied to be riding in the wagon. Anyone could handle the colt, and it did not appear afraid, though its mother would act very strange, showing her teeth, flattening her ears, and keeping her distance from us.

I rode into Fort Saskatchewan to pick up the mail on an albino gelding that was pure white with fawn tips on his ears and one black patch on his rump, about the size of a silver dollar. The horse's name was Whiteman. He was four years old and green-broken. Whiteman's mother was an Indian pony, born on the G Dot reserve in Montana. This horse had a very good disposition but had a lonesome nature. He would work faithfully when with the herd of horses, but when he was away from them, he would whinny like a suckling colt that had strayed from its mother. Quite often he would rear, plunge, and whirl. When the driver of a car would stop to speak to me, Whiteman was quite likely to buck and jump a little, and then climb on top of the car.

On the way to the post office, I passed the big penitentiary buildings, where I could see crowds of men cutting grass with shears. One prisoner shouted, "Drop a little tobacco there, Mac." Other prisoners sat on the ground and opened their mouths like birds, motioning for Copenhagen. Some of this crowd could not speak our language but had no trouble with the sign language for tobacco, which they were denied.

A guard in uniform was riding herd on foot over this bunch of prisoners. He was packing a big six-shooter in his holster that resembled Whalebone's Luger. He obviously meant business. I rode beside these fellows, who looked as if they were praying for tobacco and snuff, for a quarter of a mile. I guess they were hoping I was Santa Claus on a white horse.

After I found the post office and collected our mail, I rode around to look over the bridge that crossed the North Saskatchewan River. I found a busy highway, as Edmonton was a whopping big city just a few miles up the road. Cars were coming and going in a steady stream. The bridge was built similar to a large T. One road went over the T at the top end, going east and west. The other road crossed the bridge and continued to the south. It was a very busy spot with only an acre or two of open ground beside the river, near the bridge, where we could hold the herd of horses. As I rode back to camp to tell the boys, I was hoping the traffic would dwindle down by the time we arrived there.

We ate dinner, read our letters, and talked about the best way to cross the river. Every member of the crew felt a great responsibility for the part they were to play in crossing that bridge.

Little Bill asked, "Curly, do you intend to go through Edmonton? We'll have our pictures in the paper this time. Why don't you go in and tell the world we're coming? Anyway, we should have a real audience watching us go over this bridge today."

Little Bill mounted his roan mare. She was his best cutting horse, well trained for dodging, similar to a well-trained sheep dog. He sat in his saddle with renewed happiness after reading the good news from home. His sister had told him that by the time we landed in British Columbia, his family would be there, too. Everyone at home was well, and they were always glad to get his letters.

Later, Little Bill sat watching the traffic zip by over the end of the bridge, while his roan mare stood as still as a statue. He was singing and yodelling as though he hadn't a care in the world. The echo of his voice carried up and down this big river valley and seemed to bounce back and forth among the trees.

Rawhide was also riding a good horse. Crossing a bridge like this with a bunch of horses required a fair cowboy who was well mounted. He was sitting on his horse on the opposite side of the highway from Little Bill. Instead of singing, he was counting cars to see how many, per minute, were passing. He was trying to figure out if the traffic was getting worse or better. The herd was being held near the end of the bridge, close to the river.

Whalebone and I were considering how to handle the situation.

Herding horses on the flat, open prairie was easy compared to trailing a herd through forest and muskeg. *Courtesy Don Shapley*

We couldn't think of swimming the horses across here because they could never climb up the far side. If we waited for moonlight, we'd never get them onto the bridge, even if traffic stopped entirely. After about five hours of waiting and wondering, we decided that we had as much right to use this bridge as the cars did.

"I'm going to ride my horse across the bridge through all this traffic," I said. "I hope he doesn't jump over the side. It's a long way down to the water, and I can't swim. Whalebone, you and the boys be ready. Watch me closely, all the way across. If anyone tries to deliberately spook my horse off the bridge, you fellows nail him on this end. We're going over this bridge with these horses come heel flies or high water. I'm depending on you from this end."

I walked over to my white horse and mounted him.

"Whalebone," I called, "if I ever get Whiteman across the bridge, I'm going to put on a stampede of my own. If I can stop two or three cars for half a minute, then nothing else can get by them."

Whalebone let out a big whoop, "Curly, you dang old rang-a-tang, you're at the top of the class. If your Whiteman can't stop a car when he starts to whinny, rear, and whirl, then they must be in one heck of a hurry. He'll paw the front end off a car if it doesn't stop. Good luck to you, cowboy. Now you're entirely on your own."

I gave a few orders. "Tell the boys that when I wave my hat, they are to put the horses onto the bridge. Make a road block here, too. So long, old pard."

When I saw a big-enough gap at the end of the bridge for my horse to enter, I gently spurred Whiteman into the traffic and went across the bridge. I said to him, "The way my knees are rattling, it's no wonder you're so nervous. I hope we can hold the traffic long enough to let the horses get started across. Then it'll be up to the travellers as to what they do."

From the north side of the bridge, I could see the traffic on the Edmonton road for about fifty rods, and then the road turned behind some trees. I thought about how lucky I was to get across the bridge in this kind of traffic.

I stopped Whiteman on the highway as close to the side as possible. Cars zipped past going east, others were going west, and many from the south were going east or west. Drivers waved their hands and children waved big balloons of various colours, shouting at the white horse and me. It looked like the fourth of July, and I wondered, Do all these people know where they're going? If they do, they sure have me beat. I don't even know where we'll camp tonight.

The heaviest traffic seemed to be from the west. I sat quietly on my nervous horse, waiting for the traffic to slacken before starting the hold-up. When the moment came, the white horse plunged away from the curb and into the middle of the road. He whinnied for the horses across the river and tried to run back to them. I checked his run and turned him toward the west. Whiteman reared, whirled, and pawed his front feet in the air, while I gently spurred him on. The first car slowed and ducked around me. I seemed to be all over the road in a second or two. Two cars stopped and I waved my hat, shouting as loud as I could, "There's a herd of horses on that bridge. Please hold for a minute!"

In a short time, I could see cars stopped at the turn in the road. Some people were walking toward me and Whiteman, who was still performing.

"Is this a hold-up?" someone asked.

"Oh no, nothing like that. There's a big herd of horses on the bridge."

The travellers could not see the horses, but could soon hear the clatter of galloping hooves as the leaders came into sight. Encouraging shouts were heard from the riders.

Most people did not want to risk an accident on a bridge over a pond of water as large as the North Saskatchewan River. Some men did some mild cussing, others were swearing slightly at my horse, while those at the front end of the blockade were perfectly satisfied to wait until the horses crossed.

The boys on the south side of the bridge were an anxious lot. When they saw me wave my hat, they went to work. As soon as they had spooked a few of the leaders onto the bridge, they shouted and whooped like wildmen. It was a very exciting affair for the young riders. They followed closely so none of the horses could turn back.

In less than an hour, everything was across the bridge except the wagons.

Nobody knew how many people had waited. When the jam of cars started rolling down the road again, each car took its turn. Whiteman wasn't nearly so silly when the horses came to meet him. We waved our thanks and farewells as we pushed the herd north off the highway bridge toward a narrow trail among the trees.

The horse-trailing crew was a hungry bunch by the time we found a camping spot that night. It was a very poor place for so many horses, as the trees were thick and the grass scanty.

Rawhide rode his horse in a big circle among the trees, looking for grass and water, and Little Bill stayed with the herd. The rest of us set up camp and helped the cook get something ready to eat.

All hands could hear Rawhide shouting to Little Bill beyond the trees. "There's not much grass for the stock, but I think this place will be a quiet camp spot. At least there're no railroad tracks nearby, and a car could not get in here no how."

As the boys talked back and forth through the trees, Little Bill asked, "Do you remember the night the chuck wagon got itself lost? I'm about as hungry as a man can get, and I've been starving for three hours. It's been past dark for a long time. I hope Whalebone has plenty of dry wood in his wagon, and that he scrambles that big iron skillet full of eggs like he does sometimes."

Whalebone
Lands
in the Hospital

A RE YOU SURE WE'RE HEADING TOWARD ATHABASKA?"
Whalebone asked. "That's a heck of a long way north, and I
don't know my directions very good in these trees."

"We'll keep in sight of the telegraph lines so we don't get lost,"
I answered. "Surely someone must live up this way. Maybe they all
live in Edmonton and were all out for a car ride yesterday."

Whalebone laughed loudly. "We're far better on a lonely trail
with this bunch of broncs, but this is a terribly bumpy road to ride
a wagon on for a hundred miles. These wagons will have to be
greased again at noon today. One wheel always starts to squeak
after a day or two on the trail. Where do we get our next supplies for
the chuck box?"

"What are you short of now?"

"A crate of eggs only lasts a couple of days. I have enough bacon
until we get to Athabaska and lots of beans, prunes, spuds, and
flour."

It was early afternoon when the chuck wagon came to a creek
flowing east. Its banks had small trees, and the water was clear and
shallow, showing a solid gravel bottom. This was an ideal spot to
set up camp, shady and picturesque.

After supper, the boys took their rifles and went hunting for partridge. They had fun, and brought in some fresh meat, with plenty left over for the next day.

"Cook, you can save on your bacon now," Little Bill bragged. "We'll bring in some fresh meat every day. We can also catch fresh fish."

"Whalebone, someday I'd like to hunt with your Luger to see what it's like," said Rawhide. "I guess it wouldn't be very good for partridge. Maybe all I'd bring in would be feathers."

"When you shoot grouse, just shoot off their heads so you don't destroy the meat," replied Whalebone. "The best way to sight on a target is to aim directly below it, gradually raise your gun until the sight is straight on it, and then, bang, away goes the chicken's head."

The next day, about noon, the mosquitoes were swarming something terrible, and the outfit passed some muskeg. We cut little branches off the trees to whip the mosquitoes from our necks and faces, and our saddle horses.

These pests seemed about three times larger than the mosquitoes back home. One dive with their harpoon and a fellow's blood was leaving him. The horses were switching their tails continually. Running opposition to the pesky mosquitoes were the deer flies. They could bite like an ugly dog. When one lit on you, it stayed until its belly was full, unless it was swatted away. They would drive their suction hose through thick horse hair and try to pump a horse dry.

The weather stayed very hot, and some days there was no breeze at all. Occasionally, farms were visible, but most times their buildings were hidden in the trees.

Our muskeg troubles started when two saddle horses bogged at a noon stop. They had walked toward the water for a drink when, kerplunk, they dropped through the ground. Only their heads were showing. We made many paths in the grass before we found them. Pulling muskegs was a new experience for all of us, but we learned all we needed to know after travelling through what we called "no man's land."

This muskeg was not a large one, which was a big advantage.

When one of the horses swam within reach of my lariat, I roped it by the neck. Enough ropes and chains were linked together to reach solid ground, where the team was able to pull without bogging itself. Both bogged horses were hauled far enough away from the mire hole so they would not fall back in.

My Whiteman was pulled out of the muskeg, along with one of Rawhide's ponies. His white hide looked the same colour as the other horse's—like an elephant's. It took some currying when they were dry before a saddle could be placed on their backs again.

That night, Whalebone awoke in the middle of the night in much distress. "Curly," he shouted, "wake up. My throat feels like a branding fire."

I scrambled around in the light of the moon and northern lights until I found a cup. Then I mixed a spoonful of salt in a cup of water to make a gargle.

"Sit on the wagon pole while I look at your throat with the light of a match," I told him. "Have you ever gargled with salt and water? Try this mixture. Throw your head as far back as it will go and gargle until this cup is empty. I can't see very good, but what I can see looks bad. If this gargle doesn't help you before morning, I'll paint you all around with iodine."

Whalebone didn't sleep any more that night. About four o'clock in the morning, he was shouting hoarsely, "Roll out you rang-a-tangs, breakfast is ready. If it wasn't for me and the dog, you fellows would sleep all the time."

When Whalebone tried to eat breakfast, he couldn't swallow a bite. The inside of his throat was so red and swollen it looked like beef steak, and he was in a bad way from pain.

"I'll fix you up a little gruel-like porridge," I told him. "Maybe you can drink it if it's thin enough."

When the gruel was prepared, we all watched Whalebone try his best to drink it. This swallowing caused him a great deal of pain, and after several attempts, he gave up. He cussed a blue streak and heaved the dish, spoon, and gruel away.

"Cowboy, if I knew where to find a doctor, I'd put you on a horse and take you there. I think we must be about seventy miles from

Edmonton and fifty or more from Athabaska. What do you suggest we do?" I asked him.

Whalebone cussed and grumbled from the pain and then said, "I guess I'll live. You can't kill a cowpoke with a sore throat. If it doesn't get better soon, I'll see a doctor in Athabaska."

I looked through the cupboard in the chuck wagon and found my first-aid kit, then I fumbled through everything until I came across a bottle of iodine and of mercurochrome. I sat Whalebone on the wagon pole with his head turned back against the wagon box so the light would shine into his open mouth.

"Whatever you have, you must have had it for a week. I'm no dang doctor, but this looks like what they call septic throat. I'm going to swab it good with this red stuff, and then I'll paint the outside with iodine. This won't hurt you any."

I took my knife from my pocket, opened the small blade, and felt the sharp edge with my thumb.

Whalebone shouted, "Good Lord, man, you don't have to lance it, do you?"

I chuckled. "Oh no, not yet at least. We'll try this dope first."

I started whittling a stick to make a swab for his throat painting. When the painting job was finished, the inside of the cook's throat was well daubed, and the outside was iodined from the bottom of one ear to the bottom of the other.

I grinned and whispered, "Your tough old hide has such a heavy tan that nothing could ever blister it. I hope this helps. We'll have to do this about three times a day until it's better, or until a doctor has a chance to do something different."

All hands took a turn at cooking, but most of it was left up to me. Whalebone could not even eat thin soup, and he was running a high temperature. Cigarette smoke irritated his throat terribly, and to his disgust, he could not even chew tobacco.

"Did you take his temperature, Curly?" Little Bill asked. "Do you think our cook is in serious trouble?"

"I have nothing to take his temperature with, but I felt his head and pulse. His head will burn right off if we can't stop his fever soon. If his constitution was not similar to that of a Hereford bull, I'd say he might not make it to Athabaska in time. I'm hoping we find a hospital and doctor there. I'd hate to have to lance his throat myself, with nothing to put him asleep and you fellows holding him down like a calf at branding time. None of you would like that."

Little Bill drove the chuck wagon, making the best possible speed he could over the bumpy road. Whalebone was kept on a bed roll with wet cloths on his head. At times he raved from the fever and mumbled words that Little Bill could not understand. Everyone was very concerned.

When the chuck wagon rolled into Athabaska, the horse herd was left under Rawhide's care a few miles out of town. Big George tied his team to the wagon wheel and lay down in the shade of a tree, his dog beside him. I rode into town to make arrangements for a doctor and a hospital bed for Whalebone, while Little Bill drove the covered wagon into town at a smart pace with Whalebone bedded down inside. When they got there, the cook was able to walk into the doctor's office on his own power.

The doctor was a fairly young man. He was tall, heavy, and wore a thin-line moustache. He gave the impression that he knew his business and would have no fooling around. He asked me many questions about Whalebone's sickness. He spoke like some cranky old man until he found out a few facts.

"Do you know this man is in serious condition?" he said. "His temperature is 103°. Why did he not see a doctor before?"

"The man is from southern Saskatchewan," I replied, "way down beside the Montana border. He's been cooking on a round-up wagon on the trail since early July. He started to complain about his throat about a week ago. We doctored him as best we could and brought him here to you on a bed roll, in a covered wagon."

"What did you do for him in the last three or four days?" the doctor asked.

"Well, Doc, I'll admit we're very poor nurses. I've been painting the inside of his throat with mercurochrome three times a day. I painted the outside, three times a day, with iodine. We've kept wet cloths on his head night and day, ever since he started to show a fever. He has not eaten a bite since his throat got real sore."

The doctor smiled and got over being annoyed. "You should have been a doctor," he said. "That's about all I could have done had I been situated like you were."

When I saw Whalebone safely in a hospital bed under the doctor's care with two nurses hustling around him, my worry lessened.

"Pay strict attention to the nurses," I told Whalebone, "but don't fall in love with them." We talked seriously for a few minutes, and I explained, "We're going to camp somewhere close to town, wherever we can find a camping spot with enough grass to do us. We'll build a corral close to water and break some more saddle horses. Our time won't be lost, and you get well as soon as you can. We'll ride in here every day to see you and keep you posted on our horse-breaking activities."

With that, I left him in the care of the nurses.

Dangerous
Work

ATHABASKA WAS A VERY NICE PLACE. THE TOWN WAS
situated at the end of the railroad, more than a hundred miles
northeast of Edmonton, near the Athabaska River, in picturesque,
rugged country. Moose, bear, and other big game made their homes
there. In earlier days it had been a trapper's paradise. Now, settlers
were locating homesteads all over the country with intentions of
cutting down all the trees to make farms for the coming generations.
Athabaska had good schools, a fair-sized hospital, and other government buildings.

The people of the North country were friendly, even though
during the depression years they had little or no money. The folks
in the country were living on the natural resources of the land. They
could get wild game for meat, plenty of fish, lots of wood, water,
and berries, as well as wild honey. Good trees, for building homes,
grew everywhere. Bear meat was considered an adequate source of
fat for lard and bacon. If a settler could shoot, he could live there.

After I left Whalebone at the hospital, I went in search of Little
Bill and the chuck wagon. I found the wagon backed up in front of
a store. Little Bill was loading enough groceries to last nearly
another month on the trail. Two sacks of flour were placed under
the big tarp, and beans, spuds, dried fruit, and bacon were packed
away in cardboard boxes.

I paid for the groceries and told Little Bill, "Wait at the store while I go back for the horses. You can lead the procession through town."

I left town with my horse at a high lope. I was anxious to find out how Rawhide was handling the herd all alone. He had been left near railroad tracks in a very poor camping spot. I had to smile when I saw the millions of mosquitoes swarming over Big George, who was still sleeping restfully.

Rawhide was full of questions as we got the herd on the move toward town. "Surely we don't have to drive these horses through town, do we? I'm afraid to think of our night at Swift Current, when part of the herd took to the railway tracks, some east and some west. And then we had three riders!"

"The Athabaska River is on the north side of town, and they have a railroad yard there, too," I told him. "I've looked it over some. We'll have to travel west now. Little Bill is mapping out how to cross the town. You had just as well put on your best smile for the camera man, but don't forget, we are just two boys, and this should be a job for three good men."

When we reached town, Little Bill joined us with the chuck wagon and took the lead. Big George followed close behind. The baby colt was whinnying from the back of Big George's wagon, while the old Flying U mare tramped close behind. Rawhide and I trailed the herd as it followed the mare.

Cars honked and people cheered. Children followed on foot and bicycles. It looked as if the town was out to see Hoot Gibson of picture-show fame. Some children followed for half a mile, and we heard them shouting, "These cowboys have spurs and big hats, just like the fellows in the picture show on Saturday night."

The trail was known as the Peace River Drag. The Mountie at Empress had mentioned it, saying it was the only trail leading westward to the Peace River country.

West of Athabaska, we could see small farms and thousands, perhaps millions, of trees, and the Athabaska River to the right of the trail. On our left, the forest was so dense that a rabbit might get itself lost.

"This is a sample of the North country. We'll have from six to eight hundred miles of this, depending on how straight we can go," I remarked. "According to the map, we have to go a long way north yet and wind back and forth—perhaps to bypass mountains or impassable rivers. It shows a railroad going northwest from Edmonton and crossing the Athabaska River about sixty miles west of here. We can be sure we won't have any railroad troubles for the next sixty miles. When we reach Mirror Landing, we'll have to ferry the horses."

"Where are all the Indians we've heard so much about?" Little Bill wanted to know.

Big George replied, "The woods are full of them. Just look at this map. One reserve after another."

Little Bill took the map and laid it across his saddle. "Here is the Lesser Slave Lake. Wow, what a big puddle. On this map, it looks big enough to be part of the ocean. These rivers look powerfully big, too, but that lake must be a hundred miles long. I wonder how close we'll get to it. I'd sure like to catch some fish in there. We either have no water at all, or oceans of it. No wood at all, or forests too thick for a mouse."

Rawhide looked at the forest on both sides of the trail and exclaimed, "What are our horses going to live on through these forests if we can't find an open meadow?"

I smiled. "If a horse could wiggle in among these trees, it would find a plant called vetch. Many call it wild peavine. It grows with runners, like the peas in mother's garden. These runners cling to the trees and grow six feet high. But we'll find small meadows occasionally and let our stock fill up."

When the outfit had travelled about three miles west of town, I noticed some open spots where the road had been widened by the road builders. To my right, I could see a good place to descend the steep bank to the Athabaska River. It was a nice sandy place for the stock to get water.

"Hold it a minute, boys. Let's investigate. This looks like a place to camp for a few days. Lots of water, fresh from the mountains, and enough grass for two days."

The Peace River Drag made a turn near a loop in the river. Fires had burned off a few acres, and we could see for about half a mile. Grass, such as red top, grew along the roadside. To the north toward the river, the elevation dropped two or three hundred feet to the river valley. On the south side of the trail, road builders had chopped down a lot of trees, making the forests as even as the side of a house. We made our camp close to these trees.

"Boys," I said, "we must be three or four miles from town. We have enough range here for a few days, and this forest is full of peavine if we need it bad enough. The Indians use such pastures all the time. They just put bells on their horses' necks and turn them loose."

Rawhide gave a snort. "If our horses ever get into a place like that they'll sure need a bell. I think we'd all need to wear a bell if we went in there. I doubt if these confounded mosquitoes could even find a horse in a place like that."

"What do you say about getting your axe and building a corral down there by the river?" I asked Big George. "It would be away from the wind and all the traffic. We can cut poles and spike them to the trees and put other poles up for bars instead of a gate. Make it big enough to hold two or three hundred head. You're the lumberjack of the crew, so I'd like you to oversee this project. If we have a pen for the stock, no one will have to night herd, and everyone can have a good rest."

While the lads were hustling around to find enough tools to make a corral, I said, "If any of you wranglers wants to look after the cook house, I'm a lumberjack, too."

Three voices sounded at once, "Curly, you're elected to the chuck wagon until our old cook gets back on the job."

The horses grazed contentedly on the red top, while all hands worked to build the corral, and I turned my attention to the stove. The first supper I prepared at the new campsite was no fancy dish, but a powerful lot of food. I called from the top of the river bank, "Come and get it, boys!"

The fellows soon dropped their tools and followed one another up the steep climb to the camp. They were all puffing from the exertion and swatting mosquitoes with both hands.

Through the smoke of the mosquito smudge I had started, the crew could see a pile of hotcakes made from Whalebone's sourdough crock. The boys were in the habit of taking their meals cowboy style. The cupboard that was built into the back end of the wagon box had a door about four feet wide and five feet long. When it was let down it was like a table with two legs. Hinges fastened the cupboard to the opposite end, and kettles of prepared food and dishes were placed on the table. All hands would wash in a tin wash basin beside the wagon, and then each man would take a plate, cup, knife, fork, and spoon from the table and proceed to fill up his plate. They would sit on the wagon pole or cross-legged on the ground and fill their stomachs.

I had also half-filled a big iron skillet with scrambled eggs. When the eggs were finished, I took a butcher knife and cut the works into five slices, like a pie. Little Bill was watching closely. He smiled as he said, "You must be reserving a piece for Whalebone. There are only four of us tonight."

"I didn't cut this for Whalebone. It's for our old black dog. Whalebone always gives the dog an equal share. The dog can tell when he gets enough to eat, but with us fellows, we're never sure. Lately, we're hungry all the time."

We kept a smudge burning beside the tent that night. If the pesky mosquitoes started to swarm inside the tent, we would carry the smudge inside and drive them out. The horse herd was safely corralled inside the new pen. With no worries for the night, we went to bed.

When the camp began to stir the next morning, I rolled out and made breakfast. Shortly after daylight, Rawhide opened the bars to let the horses out to graze. After breakfast, he planned to wrangle a few head back into the corral, where he and I would get to work. As he rode back to camp for his breakfast, he was thinking about which horses would make good saddle stock.

When Rawhide reached the wagon, he shouted, "How about the Flying Dutchman for you, Curly? I'm going to start that nice brown mare with the big forty-four brand. Those two should give us a start. Building that pen was a brainwave, but it would be much handier

A typical cowboy chuckwagon. *Glenbow Archives NA-692-21*

if it had a gate on there instead of those bars. They're going to be unhandy for us when we have to sort out the horses."

When breakfast was over, and the dishes were washed and put away, all hands sat around camp and discussed many things of importance. Little Bill was worried about the baby colt. He thought it might forget us entirely if we had to camp very long. We decided to catch the colt every day and play with it as usual.

Rawhide asked Big George, "How are your wagon horses standing up to the miles of work? We might break a few more while we're here."

"I don't know how Whalebone is fixed, but mine are all right," Big George answered. "I still have my big bay mare that has never been hitched yet on this trip. She's a lovely animal—when she'll work—but she's a bit balky when I first hitch her up. I'll pick her one of these days for a change. She's fat and as gentle as a lamb."

Rawhide was getting ready to ride out to the herd. "Do you want the Flying Dutchman, Curly?"

"Sure, I want him. Bring him in. He's half-broken now. Big George and Little Bill will have to do the housework and take care of the herd today while we play with those broncs. I hope we can gentle one of them enough so we can ride him into town this afternoon to see Whalebone. One of us has to ride our best horse to take care of the man on the bronc. We don't want a runaway, or anyone in town getting hurt from our horses. We don't want to pay any fines, either. We'll flip a coin to see which one of us rides the green horse to town today."

"Do it now, Curly," shouted Little Bill. "Heads rides the Flying Dutchman." He flipped a coin high into the air, then walked over and picked it up. "Tails, Rawhide. That's you."

I called to Rawhide, "Wait another minute while I saddle a horse. I'll go along and give you a hand. We'll bring a fresh horse in for Little Bill, and this pair can go with the herd."

"Roll your spurs if we're going to gentle a horse to ride into town this afternoon," Rawhide said. "You'll be riding Captain, I suppose. We'd better bring him in now. We'll put on a wild west show down there in that valley, and no one will see it except you and me."

We picked the horses we wanted and brought in seven or eight extras to the corral.

"I'll saddle my old favourite and rope that brown mare of yours," I told Rawhide. "We'll put a hackamore on her head and tie her to a tree. I'll rope the Flying Dutchman, and we'll tie him to another tree. Then we can drop the gate bars and turn these extras out again. Our day's work is about to begin. Be mighty careful, cowboy. We don't want to get hurt. That hospital looked full yesterday. So don't take a lot of fool chances. Between ourselves and the Indians, we'll have to look after ourselves."

The antics of the two broncs once the rest of the bunch were let out would have been great material for a moving-picture camera. Rawhide's brown mare rolled on the ground like a trained dog. She twisted the nose band of her hackamore until she was sneezing and choking. She would jump to her feet and pull like a wild cat, then throw herself and choke some more. We hustled around, trying to untie the rope, which was as tight as a fiddle string.

Rawhide whispered, "That brown mare was never halter-broken. She's a real hot-blooded cuss. After your grey took four or five good pulls, he remembered that you had handled him once before. He has a good head and a great body, but this brown mare looks like a scatterbrain to me. Just look at the white in her eyes. If I can ride her at all, I'll put some miles on her right here in this pen. If she was to stampede toward the woods, across that road, she would brush me off in one heck of a hurry."

"That's what I got old Cap here for, she won't get a rod away. Don't worry about being scraped off. If she's that tough, I'll pick you off and let her go," I told him.

Rawhide put on that wicked little grin that was so becoming on him. He had a happy twinkle in his eye when the brown mare showed signs of leading on a catch rope.

"We'd better sack these horses out good while we have the time and place to do it," I exclaimed. "I'm going to tie up a hind foot on my grey and go all over his body with a curry comb. I'll even put something under his tail like a crupper. Did you ever have a horse switch his tail over your rope and blow up when you were dallied hard and fast with a cow or calf on the end of your rope? That's because the nerves of his tail were not trained. They have so much power in their tail that no man could pull the rope out. It's things like that that get a cowboy killed. He gets twisted up in his own rope on a horse gone hog wild, all because the horse's nerves were not properly trained. It's too bad we don't have time for the job when we find a good place to work them out. I don't blame a horse for unwinding with us when all the time we have is to snub him down, crawl on, and hope for the best."

Rawhide went to the wagon and returned with a heavy, soft rope. Soon we had the mare's hind foot held in such a fashion that she was just able to place her toe on the ground to hold her weight. Rawhide stood behind the disabled foot so he would not get kicked, then commenced to trim her long tail.

"I remember one time, about ten years ago, down beside the Montana border, along the forty-ninth parallel," I recalled. "I was alone, trying to ride a big clunk of a horse that my boss had got in a horse trade. It was my job to start him. I heard afterward that this horse had been used in the rodeos. I had no time to educate him, as we were making a roundup that afternoon. I was hustling all I could, thinking about the horse and forgetting everything else. One side of the corral was a cow shed made of lumber that was standing upright. It had two doors about six feet high. I put a plank across one of the doors, near the end of the corral, where I was working with the horse. I forgot entirely about the other door farther down. When I first tried to mount this big rough cuss, he threw his head down and whirled to the right. I had my left hand on the nose band of his halter. My left foot was in the stirrup, and my right hand was on the saddle horn, only half-mounted. When I threw my right leg over the saddle, he whirled back to the left and really bucked. My right spur struck his shoulder several times while I was pawing to find a stirrup. I never did find my stirrup. My spur strap broke, and did I take an airplane ride."

Rawhide sat down on the ground and laughed long and loud. It must have reminded him of some of his experiences. After he stopped laughing, he asked, "What became of you then?"

I chuckled as the memory of the incident came back. "Well, the corral was a real mud hole after a June rain. It hadn't been cleaned for a year and was all sloppy manure." I laughed again and said, "When I left that saddle, I turned a complete flip in the air and landed sitting up in cow manure that soon ran into my pockets. That old bronc jumped over top of me. He didn't touch me, but I could feel one foot mighty close to my head. The next jump that horse made took him through that cow-shed door. The saddle horn didn't miss the top by more than an inch. I sat there watching him, very pleased to be sitting in the slush of the corral."

We got busy with our horses once again. I was silent for a few minutes, watching the performance of the two horses in the pen as they coped with having a back foot tied up. Suddenly I said, "Rawhide, you know, I shouldn't be monkeying around with horses at all. I have a wife and daughter back home. They're looking for me to come back all in one piece and alive. I'm going to tell you a secret—sometime before Christmas, I am hoping to become a daddy again."

Rawhide shouted, "Good luck to you, partner. I hope it's a little cowboy."

Sometime that forenoon, while the new saddle horses were having a breather, we were chatting again. I asked Rawhide, "What do you intend to do with yourself for a life career?"

Rawhide looked surprised and said, "Why, Curly, if we ever get our outfits landed and located in that unsurveyed country of British Columbia, I'm going to have the biggest horse ranch in that whole territory. If Little Bill's folks get moved out there and if his sister likes the climate, Little Bill and I will be partners. We have a brand picked out for our outfit. It will be a TC on the left hip. I know you'll have to go back home, Curly, but what do you intend to do for the rest of your life?"

I replied, "After we get properly located with camps built and arrangements made for feed for the stock, I'll go back. Who knows, after this depression is over—if it ever is—and drought quits the south country so it can rain occasionally, I may run a few cows back there again. If it wasn't for the drought, that's the best ranch country in the world. At least the best I've ever seen. Someday I'd like to own a herd of purebred Herefords, the best in the west. If we don't all get into a muskeg, killed by a bear, or a falling tree, or maybe a horse, I may even write a book about the toughest wranglers of the century: Rawhide, Whalebone, Little Bill, and Big George."

Rawhide laughed and said, "If you do, don't forget to mention Curly and his Flying Dutchman."

Nervous Horses

....

TIME PASSED QUICKLY AS WE WORKED WITH THE HORSES in the temporary corral along the Athabaska River that morning. We had ridden the grey and the brown for some time. The brown mare had thrown herself twice in a rage, but Rawhide had a knack for getting clear, and always bounced away from her. He was saying very little and looked as if he had something on his mind. But he was still smiling.

A good slicking out certainly helped the Flying Dutchman. He now behaved in a civilized manner, considering how he could pitch when he really got started. I must have ridden him a few miles in the corral when I heard Little Bill shouting from the top of the hill. "Dinner has been ready for at least an hour, and that hospital in town must have special visiting hours. You better roll up your spurs."

I took the saddle off the grey gelding, gave him a love pat on the neck, then turned him out of the corral to graze his dinner. I threw his saddle upside-down on the ground and placed his saddle blanket over top to dry in the sun. I led Captain over to a choice piece of grass and hobbled him, then climbed the steep hillside to the chuck wagon.

Little Bill, as cook, was scolding us because we had kept dinner waiting. In a faked, snarling voice, he said, "I can't keep anything hot unless it's heated in the sun. When you fellows get off alone doing nothing, you always forget to come back."

Rawhide emptied the wash basin and eyed Little Bill as he answered, "What do you mean nothing—my brown mare is worth another fifty dollars today. When we get back from town, she'll be worth another fifty. That's not peanuts for our crew, and you say doing nothing?" He smiled, picked up a plate from the table, and loaded it to the top.

When Rawhide and I reached town that afternoon, we hunted for a quiet spot to leave our horses while we went to visit Whalebone. Rawhide tied his brown mare to the horn of my saddle, in what we thought was an out-of-the-way corner.

I went to see Whalebone's doctor first and asked about his new patient.

"He's doing fine. You'd better go in and see him. His fever has gone down some, and he talks of you all the time. He told me that you intended to lance his throat. Now what about that?"

I grinned and answered, "That'd be the last thing I'd like to do, but I'd never have allowed it to break and go into his system if it was an abscess. I thought it would come to a head of some kind. I certainly didn't want that kind of a job out there in no man's land. Did you have to lance it?"

The doctor nodded his head and said, "Yes, the treatment you gave him brought it to a head. I lanced it this morning. He's eating some today. If his fever stays down, he'll be in fairly good shape inside of a week. Go and see him, and stay as long as you like. Tell the nurses that I said so."

Our spurs jingled as we walked down the hospital hall to Whalebone's room. A nurse was laughing at something Whalebone was telling her. When she saw us, she said, "This is the first prairie cowboy we've had for a patient since I started working here three years ago. He just told me that he was worrying about a crew of horse wranglers that may not be getting enough to eat until he gets back on the job. He told me all about Saskatchewan and Montana and has promised to tell me about the muskegs of our fair Alberta. I can't believe it's possible to trail horses so far."

"We're not halfway yet," said Rawhide. "One mile in the bush is about equal to two or three miles on the open prairie."

I laughed with the nurse and said, "If you have to inoculate this old cowboy, you may have to file a sharp point on the needle. His hide is about as thick as a harness trace. Even these big mosquitoes can't penetrate his carcass."

When the nurse left, Whalebone sat up in bed. He looked lonesome in this big, bright room.

"How do you like a clean, soft bed for a change?" I asked.

"It looks nice, Curly, but I didn't sleep very good last night. Too many windows, and it's daylight all night in this country. Did you fellows notice that it never got real dark last night?"

"That was the northern lights," I explained. "Just wait until we get a little farther north, we'll see the midnight sun. I've read Robert Service's poems of the North country and all his stories. I didn't believe them, but we'll see for ourselves in another two weeks."

Whalebone was very glad we had come to visit. He inquired about Big George and Little Bill and hoped that they would catch up on some sleep now that they had a pen for the stock to stay in at night.

"Big George is thinking about taking a holiday," I said. "An old friend of ours, from the Val Marie country, lives close to Athabaska on a homestead. Maybe you knew him. He's one of the Clement boys. We call him Albert. I'll find out which direction he lives from town. Big George can take my Pigeon mare and have a good visit. No doubt he'll go on a bit of a spree while he's gone, but he'll enjoy a day or two away. He has nothing to do at camp. If we didn't have some horses to break, I'd like to see Albert myself. He used to be one of the best trick ropers in the South country."

Whalebone replied, "Oh yes, I know him."

Rawhide described to Whalebone the horse-breaking activities of the forenoon. "I rode my forty-four mare into town today for the first time. I left her tied to Curly's horse. I hope she's still there. Curly calls her a cowboy killer because she likes to throw herself when her temper gets the best of her. She's the easiest-gaited horse I've ever ridden. She can walk five miles an hour and, oh, how smooth. She can be kind of treacherous, though. She threw herself flat twice today. Remember the Flying Dutchman? Curly has spent the forenoon on that horse, and tomorrow when we come to visit you, he'll be riding him."

Visiting hours at the hospital were soon over. We felt we had stayed long enough and that it was time for Whalebone to get some rest. Once again, the jingle of spurs could be heard in the hall as we left.

"I'm going to inquire at the store to see if they know of an Albert Clement," I told Rawhide. "Surely some of these merchants will know where he lives. He may even be in town today. It's important that we put the big boy on the proper trail, or he'd never find the Clement's place among all these trees. I'm more afraid of Big George getting lost than anyone else on our crew. How many times has he taken a wrong turn on the trail when he was supposed to be following the chuck wagon? He was raised in the woods in Quebec and claims to be quite a bushman, but he's lived twenty years on the prairie. I guess you can forget a lot about the bush in that amount of time."

Rawhide grinned, thinking of how many times I had back-tracked along the trail when Big George had taken a wrong turn. "The old boy is a great fellow, the biggest-hearted man I ever knew, but he's beginning to feel his age some. He would give any of us his shirt in a swarm of mosquitoes. We'll put him on the right trail tomorrow."

After I talked to a neighbour of Albert's, who gave me directions, I felt relieved.

"Why are you letting Big George ride Pigeon?" Rawhide asked. "Is she safe enough to send with him?"

"Pigeon is all right. She weighs twelve hundred pounds. Big George is 255 pounds. He would make an ordinary pony's back sag. Pigeon is a good free walker, and that's about as fast as Big George will want to travel. He'll take plenty of time and enjoy the scenery along the Athabaska River. I'm sure he'll take good care of Pigeon, too."

"Pigeon will do that all right," Rawhide said, "but she used to be quite nervous. I hear that this is bear country, and if a bear was hungry for horse meat, can you imagine what Pigeon would do with Big George? Can a bear be outrun on a horse?"

"I don't know for sure, but when I was a fairly young lad, I outran one once. I remember my brother, Bill, and I were both barefoot, and we gave that old brown cuss a run for his life."

Rawhide roared with laughter and said, "I guess it was a race for your own life."

When we were ready to return to camp, we found that our saddle horses had moved slightly, and the brown mare seemed to be very nervous. A group of youngsters, ranging in age from eight to fourteen years, had gathered to look at the horses with the big western saddles on their backs.

My Captain was standing in the middle of a back street with his reins grounded and his feet well braced. The brown mare made a few ugly pulls to get away. Rawhide walked quietly toward her and untied the taut rope. He tried to rub her neck with his hand, but she was afraid of him. Then he tried to lead her and turn her in a small circle to ease her nerves. Finally he got a hold of a stirrup and gently moved it back and forth along her side.

"Do you want me to dally her so you can mount her?" I asked.

"Oh no, she surely hasn't forgotten this morning. I think she'll let me on in a minute or two. I'll take up some slack on my cinch, and when she isn't looking, I'm going to hop on her back."

I mounted Captain and sat watching Rawhide. More people began to gather around, wondering if this was some kind of a horse trade. When Rawhide thought the time was right, he stepped quietly into the saddle. But long before Rawhide was seated, the brown mare went into fast action. She made three high buck jumps into the street and then let her legs go limp, flopping flat on her side. Rawhide tiptoed away from her without getting hurt. The mare immediately jumped to her feet. With a loud snort, she started down the street as fast as she could go, bucking with an empty saddle.

She had only gone a rod or two before I had her snubbed to my saddle. The crowd scattered in a hurry.

Rawhide shouted, "I sure hope Whalebone was watching out of his window. He'll laugh all night."

Rawhide walked to his horse once more and took a firm grip on his hackamore. He pulled the horse's head toward the stirrup and mounted her again. I jumped my horse close to the brown mare, and we galloped out of town.

I watched the way Rawhide's horse was travelling. "That mare will be a good pony after a few day's riding. We'll need more saddle horses yet before we get to British Columbia. We should keep old Baldy for a wrangler horse and nothing more. I saw him limping yesterday."

Rawhide answered, "Yes, he was lame yesterday. He had a stone in his foot, but I found it and took it out. His hooves are worn down quite smooth. He needs horseshoes. He's a tough old rascal and a good pony. Can you shoe a horse, Curly?"

"I've shoed quite a few in the last ten years. We'll shoe him tonight. No horse in our bunch needs to go lame so long as we can fit him. We have a bag full of horseshoes in the wagon."

That evening, Little Bill and Rawhide went to town and visited Whalebone and met his nurse. They also met some young folks who had watched Rawhide and his brown mare. They had an enjoyable evening.

In a few days, young folks were coming to the camp, where Little Bill entertained them with music and song. Most evenings, the camp entertained some Indian lads, too. Little Bill was all smiles when the ladies from town asked permission to take some pictures.

"Little Bill has no special girlfriend," said Rawhide, "but he has laid claim on every nice-looking lady he has seen since we left home. I'm going to learn to play that guitar and yodel like a coyote, too. Maybe then, some of those ladies will look at me."

After breakfast the next morning, Rawhide saddled Pigeon for Big George and escorted the old cowboy to town, putting him on the trail to Clement's. I sent my best regards. I would have liked to see the Clement family, but I was obliged to stay on the job.

After a few days, Whalebone began to recover from his illness. A couple of us went to see him every day, riding a green horse on the trip to town.

Once Whalebone began to eat, he was anxious to get out of the hospital. He was pale beneath his tan, revealing his several bad days of pain. He had failed in weight enough to be noticeable and was still fairly quiet.

I wrote a letter that Whalebone dictated from his bed. In it, he told his school marm:

> I am well treated in the hospital and am fit as a fiddle now. It is the doctor's orders that I can't work for a day or two yet. I had a little bit of a fever for a few days before Curly roped me and dragged me into this hospital. It is the first one that I ever had to be in overnight. I have a good doctor looking after me and good nurses. Some of the crew ride in here to see me every day.
>
> We should be in grizzly-bear country from here on west. I hope that I can get a big hide off a bear for a carpet to put in our new log house. We will have moose heads in every room, too.
>
> We will be landing with the horses within another month. The boys have been breaking a few more saddle horses for the road while they are waiting on me to get out of here. That won't take long now, as I am beginning to feel good, and I am anxious to get back on the job.

I rode the Flying Dutchman to town on occasion. Spectators gathered around each time we came. They were expecting to see a stampede, such as the brown mare had put on the first day she was ridden. Quite often, they were not disappointed. The green-broken saddle horses were always nervous in town, and the riders had to be careful that the horses did not get a good start at pitching.

The grazing ground where the herd was held was cropped quite close, and the horses now foraged in the timber for peavine. It was a terrible job to cowboy them out of the woods, as some would wander a mile back from the trail. Bears were plentiful in these woods, and we packed a gun for safety measures, hoping we would never have to use it.

We greased the wagons for the road, and everything was ready to roll as soon as Whalebone returned to his cooking job. In another day or two, we would bid Athabaska goodbye.

Pulling Muskeg

....

BIG GEORGE HAD A BIG STORY TO TELL WHEN HE RETURNED from his visit with the Clement family. "There is hardly a homesteader back that way who owns a horse. I tried to get a sale for a few horses, but no one seems to have any money. If I had offered them for ten dollars apiece, I couldn't have sold one. I thought it was tough back home, but I'm wondering how we'll make out ourselves in British Columbia.

"I was told that the woods are full of horse thieves, dog thieves, and hard-up homesteaders. We may even have to watch our chuck wagon. It could easily be robbed while we're sleeping. Somebody stole my dog while I was away, but he chewed the rope and got away. People in this country use dogs for pack horses, and I sure don't want anyone to abuse my dog."

I was wondering about what Big George had said concerning the desperate situation in the North country. I thought it would require a great deal of nerve to raid the chuck box while five men were sleeping close by in a tent.

"If a man was hungry and asked for food, we would try to fill him the best we could," I said. "If he tried to rob the chuck box, he would put us all hungry, and I wouldn't like that very much. If he stole our horses, he'd be an outlaw. If he stole the black dog, he would have the whole crew hunting for him and woe betide that fellow—we would hang his hide in a tree for an example. I hope you're mistaken about the thieves because we have met some very friendly people who stopped by to chat and appeared to be gentlemen."

I led a saddle horse with an empty saddle into town and waited at the hospital door for Whalebone. When he was released, after about eight days in bed, he was a happy lad. Two nurses stood at the hospital door and waved good cheer as Whalebone mounted his horse and we rode out of town.

Whalebone's appetite had come back with a bang. "Boys," he said, "yesterday they fed me four times, and I still went to sleep as hungry as a wolf. I'll have to shoot a deer, bear, or perhaps a small moose to fill me up again. It's too bad we don't have some ice packed on the wagon so we could store fresh meat. When we get located, I'm certainly going to build an ice house and a smoke house. We may have to eat pony and do without beef steak for a year or two until we raise some cattle, but we'll live fat, just the same as we always have."

We were all glad to have the cook back, and Rawhide and Little Bill were both trying to bring him up to date on last week's happenings.

Little Bill told him, "The grass for our horses is all gone. Lately they've wandered into that brush for half a mile, sometimes farther.

"Last Tuesday night, we had a terrific windstorm. If it wasn't for the shelter of this bunch of trees, it would have blown our tent away. I guess you saw where the corral was built, about three hundred feet down in that hole, along the river. In the middle of the night, the windstorm blew down a big tree that part of the corral was spiked to. It flew dead centre into the corral and landed among the horses. They must have come out of that pen in a terrible hurry because the bars from the gate were scattered all the way to the foot of the hill. In the morning, every horse was gone, but none were killed or crippled. We had to chop that log into five pieces to take it out of there. We can hardly corral the herd since that storm. Some of those horses are real spooked. Loading the next ferry won't be easy."

When we left the Athabaska camp, I was riding the Flying Dutchman and following the herd very well. The grey gelding would now be ridden in turn with the other saddle horses of my string. He was educated on how to neck rein properly, would allow himself to be caught, and would let a rider step on and off his back. He soon learned that a rider was supposed to land on his feet, not on his head. Before nightfall, he would know how to carry a man at least twenty-five miles a day, along with some other fundamental points.

The settlers were happy to sell a crate or two of eggs for cash instead of taking trade at the stores. Once in a while, a farmer would follow the wagon for half a day to sell eggs or fish and to trade horses.

In the days ahead, we got well acquainted with the muskegs of northern Alberta. We became experts on how to pull out mired horses.

One day an Indian lad caught a ride with Whalebone for a few miles west. As they travelled along together, Whalebone asked about the country. The cook mostly wanted to know if the boy could tell him where he could find enough grass and water for a night camp. The day's trail had already been long, hot, and dusty, and there was no grazing in sight.

The Indian boy said, "Mister, there isn't much grass along this road, but if you want to leave the trail for about two miles, my mother has a half section. It's all fenced with lots of grass."

Whalebone stopped the chuck wagon and called to me, "What do you say about leaving this trail if we find grass and water all fenced? It's another ten miles, though. Can you and the boys last that long without supper?"

I thought about another ten miles on an empty stomach. "Whalebone," I said, "if you don't find grass and water in the next ten miles, you better take the boy's offer. I'm as hungry as a wolf now, but I haven't seen enough grass in the last twenty miles to feed my pony, and I know he's hungry, too."

The hands of the clock rolled around, and the sun set. The mosquitoes sang their songs of hunger. We tightened our belts and kept on riding. Big George was weary and tired of the jolting wagon. The northern lights began to shine and dart back and forth between the sky and the earth. Still, everyone followed the chuck wagon. When we began to think that this day would never end, we saw the wagons leave the road and turn to the right. We soon became alert and turned the lead horses onto the narrow trail.

Little Bill shouted, "There's a gate. I hope this is the place."

This was another day to be remembered— at least twelve hours in the saddle. In another half-hour, we were peeling off saddles and harnesses. The colt and stove were unloaded, and we prepared to set up camp.

The tent was erected in a clearing, close to a large clump of trees, and bed rolls were soon placed around. Whalebone was short of bread, so he made a stack of hotcakes and bacon and eggs. The aroma of coffee in the open air was something to a hungry puncher.

I sang to the boys as they hustled,

A cowboy's life is a dreary, dreary life,
He's driven through the heat and cold,
While the rich man sleeps on his velvet couch,
Dreaming of his silver and gold.

The Indian boy also had a wonderful appetite that evening, and Whalebone kept piling up the hotcakes.

That night, we slept, snored, and dreamed, knowing that the horses were fenced in, but none of us had any dreams about being camped on the edge of a muskeg.

Behind the clump of trees where our tent was pitched was a muskeg that covered an entire acre. The first man out of bed the next morning noticed a grey horse swimming around and around in the muskeg. On second glance, he saw four more horses in the same situation.

"Horses in the muskeg! All hands roll out!"

The grey horse was an overgrown Percheron colt that belonged to Big George. The colt was only three years old, but he was a good-sized fellow, and was Big George's pride and joy. The other four horses were bronco mares, wild as deer and not halter-broken. These horses were swimming in the muskeg among grass that seemed to be growing on ten inches of ground—there was water under the surface of the ground. The horses were swimming with their heads out of the water and were nearly exhausted.

I looked the situation over. I knew, almost immediately, what must be done. "There's no use panicking, boys. We'll take them out one at a time. Everybody be mighty careful that you don't get in that place, too. You better hitch up old Dan and Daisy. They're our best pulling team. Rawhide, you bring the eveners from the wagon and that pile of corral rope and chains. Bring all that we have, we wouldn't dare get a team too close to this hole."

Big George felt so bad to see his prize colt in muskeg that he was almost crying. He was excited, hopping around like a schoolboy, saying, "What will we do, Curly? I'll shoot him before I leave him drown in that mud hole."

"You'd better relax," I answered. "Get your axe and chop down five or six of these small trees. Lay them over this boggy ground, end to end. I'll go out as far as I can safely go. One of you boys, go to the far side and throw branches and shout enough to scare them my way. I'll rope them by the neck, and Rawhide will haul them away, one at a time."

Big George soon made the chips fly, and by the time a good quiet pulling team was caught and ready, the fallen trees were in place. I was away out there with my rope, waiting for a horse to swim near enough to be caught.

"If I fall in here," I said, "one of you fellows better rope me by the neck and pull me out. I can't swim a stroke in clear water, much less in water and mud all mixed up."

Whalebone shouted, "We won't let you drown, Curly. I can swim like a duck."

Little Bill went around the muskeg to the far side and threw in pieces of tree limbs, making the water splash. He was yelling at the horses, "If you want to live, just swim over there to Curly."

The grey colt could barely move as he swam within reach of my lariat. I tossed my loop over his head. A tear showed in the corner of Big George's eye. When he saw the rope snare his colt, he feared that I would not be able to hold him alone, so he scrambled over to help me. Somehow he missed his footing and, in a flash, was in the muskeg.

This big boy had been a good swimmer in his younger days and was not the least bit afraid of the water. He made a fast grab for a fair-sized tree limb and hung on while he got a breath of fresh air into his lungs. He snorted like a bronc for a second or two and then struggled toward the tree.

I shouted, "Take your time. I can easily hold this horse while he's swimming." Whalebone's rope shot out with a swish and settled over the big fellow's shoulders. Big George proceeded to climb back onto the small tree.

The grey colt was pulled out and released without too much trouble. The bronco mares came out likewise, but they did not appreciate Rawhide's kindness and tried their best to paw him with their feet. Some of those mares nearly bit his hand as he held their nose high in the air to take off their neck ropes.

It was noon when we returned to camp for our breakfast. Big George put on dry clothes and hung the wet ones in the sun. The five horses were covered with the bluish green mud. It was caked on their hides so thick their brands could not be seen. We made sure the big herd stayed away from the area.

Little Bill complained to Rawhide about missing his breakfast. "We almost missed our supper last night, too," he said.

Rawhide started to laugh. "I've been watching you last night and today. It's plain to see you didn't miss any meals. You just postponed them for a few hours. I sure hope we don't have to postpone our supper like we did last night. I was nearly starved. The smell of the spruce and pine . . . my what a smell. I never ate so much in all my life."

Little Bill agreed. "When we have to wait so long for supper, I nearly starve. I guess it must be the change in climate."

It had been quite a morning. But as soon as we had packed up, we were ready for the long trail once more.

An Unwilling
Ferry Operator

THE MAP OF ALBERTA I WAS STUDYING SHOWED THE SOUTH-
ern part of the province in detail, but the northern region was
very vague. There was a railroad between Edmonton and a little
village, with the Indian name of Pouce Coupé, at the western edge of
the Peace River block of British Columbia. The spot where the
railroad crossed the Athabaska River was known as Mirror Landing.

"With luck, we should reach Mirror Landing tomorrow afternoon," I told the boys. "We'll have to ferry the horses there. We're
making good time lately—I guess that rest we had was good for man
and beast. We seem to be full of pep."

Rawhide took a squint at the map I was holding. "Do we follow
the railroad?" he asked.

"I don't know any more than you do," I told him.

"Take a look here," he said. "There's a loop turning north
through Peace River town. It's not so far across there, but if we
follow the railroad around that loop, it's three hundred miles. Why
can't we go straight and make it in one hundred?"

I grinned at Rawhide, "That'll be something for us to figure
out as we head toward the loop. I'd hate to follow a trail for a
hundred miles and then have to swim the Peace River to boot.
There are two raging Smoky Rivers in there. Let's see how we
make it over the Athabaska. Maybe our longing for adventure

will ease up some when we look down into that mile-deep puddle."

It was almost noon when Big George and Whalebone reached the heights above the Athabaska valley at Mirror Landing. While they were chaining their wagon wheels, Whalebone said, "Take a look down over the tops of those trees. Imagine what a runaway wagon would be like with a good start from here. What would be left of us? Just some hide and hair off our horses, I guess, and nothing of us. I'm fixing my wagon wheels solid with this chain so my horses have to pull real hard to drag the wagon to the bottom. I wonder how far back the boys are with the herd. If we get to the river first, we can make arrangements to ferry the horses?"

Big George and Whalebone looked long and far across the valley. They could see millions of acres of trees but no clearings— not even one big enough for a potato patch.

"I wonder who chopped the Peace River Drag all the way across this wilderness," Big George said. "How would the railroad builders find their way through those trees and muskegs? They must have had an Indian trail to follow and a crew of Indian guides. That river must be nearly half a mile wide. We'd better hustle down and do some fishing while we wait for the riders to catch up."

Whalebone continued to look in the distance. "The first explorers didn't have a wagonload of grub like we have. They each had a small birch-bark canoe, a rifle, a six gun, and a blanket. Perhaps they had a fur coat, but that's all."

"A compass must have been part of their equipment," replied Big George.

"I wouldn't believe a compass in a place like this," declared Whalebone. "I think the sun rises in the north. Anyway, it's daylight nearly all night long here."

Big George was remembering his boyhood days back east in Quebec. He thought about the old history books at school that told tales of the early settlers among the Indians. He shouted to Whalebone, "Yes, sir, the Indians have taught us all we know about living on the natural resources of the country. Still, I wouldn't want to be dumped off here all alone."

Whalebone was ready to go. He spoke to his horses and eased

the wagon down the steep hill. Instead of his usual command, he was shouting, "Slow up, you long-legged devil up there on the lead."

The cook began thinking seriously about how his life depended on the logging chain that was snubbed to the rim of the wheel. He remembered the first really bad hill, where he had chained the wagon wheels as he entered the valley of Lac Pelletier. That place had looked steep at the time—down and down, over the brakes of the South Saskatchewan River. It had nearly made his hair stand on end. Now he was wondering if his hair might turn white by the time he reached the bottom of this hill. If the chain broke or wore through, he would have no hair at all. If anything were to give way on Big George's wagon, it would run plum over top of him. Then his mind returned to the job at hand, and he shouted loudly, "Whoopee, let'er buck, ride'er cowboy!" and carefully guided his four-horse team to the bottom.

After Whalebone and Big George reached the river, they tied their horses to a wagon wheel, then waited for the horse herd to catch up. Whalebone watched the tiny ferry coming from the far side of the Athabaska River. It was the smallest ferry he had ever come upon. When it drew closer, he noticed its operator. He was one of the largest men Whalebone could remember seeing.

He whispered to Big George, "That man is almost as heavy as a cow pony. Do you suppose this is a government ferry? That outfit is not much bigger than my wagon. I'm sure I couldn't put my wagon on there with my lead team out in front. How long do you suppose it will take us to ferry our big herd across this wide river on a scow that size?"

Whalebone and Big George stood beside the river watching the water create white foam as it splashed against the ferry.

"We'd better make arrangements with the ferry operator to take our horses across," said Whalebone. "Curly must have found a grass patch somewhere and stopped to let the horses graze. Lately, he never misses a chance when he sees a small wild meadow. He likes to keep the horses' bellies full." Both men sat down on an old log and rolled a smoke while the ferry nudged into its landing place.

The ferry operator was a big jolly Indian of middle age. He reminded the two of Santa Claus because his huge tummy would jiggle up and down when he laughed. He had a very rosy complexion and looked like a picture of good health. He laughed in a good-natured way about his size. "I'm not quite so heavy now. In the hot weather, I usually come down to about 330 pounds."

This crossing looked like a lonely place to work. The ferry operator seemed glad to meet these two men with the horses and wagons. However, the smile soon left his face when Whalebone told him about the big herd of horses to be ferried across the river.

"Oh no, Mister, it can't be done. I won't take them. I'm not obliged to do so. Last week, I tried to ferry a big load of wild horses for some prairie men and nearly drowned myself. Those horses tore the sides off my scow, knocked me into the river, and jumped right off after me. I'm not over that scare yet, and I don't think I'll ever forget it. I wired to the headquarters at Edmonton about such matters, and they told me to use my own judgement and not to take chances with my life. I'm sorry, Mister, but my nerves just won't let me do that any more."

Whalebone took a chew of tobacco and began thinking. He looked at his watch and said, "The boys are slow today. I wonder what's keeping them. I think I'll walk back a ways and tell Curly that he better be prepared to swim the horses."

When Whalebone had climbed about halfway up the steep hill, he saw the horses pop into sight. He scrambled off the road and hid himself among some trees as the herd went by. When he saw me, he came over and told of his disappointment at the ferry crossing.

"Curly, I know that Indian is a fine man. He's just scared, and I don't blame him much. You may overcome it, Curly, if you work at it right. I was nearly scared myself when I brought the chuck wagon off this mountain, but I overcame that fear, and here I am in fairly good shape. If we have to swim that Athabaska River, we'll drown half our horses. We're a long way from home, but I'm sure I wouldn't want to settle with a big herd among these sticks."

Whalebone and I debated what to do, while the younger riders went on with the herd.

"What sort of place will we have to load the ferry?" I asked.

"It's the worst in the world, just a wee tiny ferry. Nothing can be done but to run the horses out onto that scow. We'll have a heck of a time if you can't persuade that big fellow to let them on. You better go down there and see what you can do. I know his mind is made up. He must have had a bad time trying to swim out among that bunch of broncs, and it's a wonder he ever made it out alive. You'd better talk to him and find out what you can do. I'll go back to the wagon and cook up a good feed. We'll fill that big belly full of coffee. It's a darn shame that Big George's crock is always empty."

The ferry operator had a feeling he was in the enemy's camp when the horse herd showed up, a quarter-mile in length. He must have been thinking, That's final. Those horses can stay here and eat brush for all I care. I wonder how these fellows ever found my ferry anyhow?

These thoughts were foremost in the ferry operator's mind when I rode up beside him and stepped down from my horse. I introduced myself. Neither of us spoke a word about ferrying the horses. I asked many questions: How long have you worked for the Alberta government? How far is the next ferry on this river? Do you find this a lonesome job? What time do you quit at night? Where do you live when you are off duty?

We talked for about twenty minutes before I brought up the subject on both our minds. I remarked, "Our wagon cook has just told me all about the bad accident you came through last week. That was a mighty close call for you. How did you manage to survive among that lot of horses anyway?"

"Those horses were really wild stock. There were eight or nine men loading the scow, while I hid behind the controls. The horses didn't want to go on the ferry and were dodging and snorting with fear. All these men were shouting in at least three different languages, and I don't suppose the horses understood one word they were saying. I hid in behind that wheel for almost an hour before the men could get any horses onto the ferry. When they did come on, there were twice too many horses for this small ferry. They jumped, reared, and tramped the sides right off the ferry, pushing me off, too. I never was so close to a bronc before in my life, and I hope I never have to get that close again."

I listened carefully as he told of his near-tragic escape. "I was in the First World War for nearly two years, and I've seen some scary things in my time. But being in the water with that bunch of horses was the worst experience of my life. I was trying to swim in that treacherous river, but the horses swam faster. They tried to climb onto my back out there, while I was near drowning. I can't exactly tell you how I got out and still had enough life left in me to crawl up onto the bank. I'll never forget it."

The man could speak good English, and I was still listening to his wild-west tale when Whalebone shouted, "Coffee's ready! Come a-running before I dump it out."

There were no travellers to be ferried across, so the ferry operator and I went to the wagon for refreshments. Whalebone had done as he said he would. Food was heaped in his kettles, and a pail of coffee was brewing on the stove. All hands talked as we ate a late dinner.

I told the ferry operator how far we had travelled and how many times we had ferried the horses since we had left home. I also told him of the system that we used with very little trouble. We found out from him that this crossing was the only ferry on the river.

When we had finished dinner, I spoke seriously to the ferry operator. "This river is far too big for us to swim. We would likely lose most of our herd, and we can't afford to do that. If we've come this far and can't cross, then our outfit is busted financially. I'd be willing to put two horses on at a time if that is the best we could do safely. I certainly don't want to make any trouble for you or ourselves, but it's important that we get across somehow."

The ferry operator was full of hot coffee and the cook's best specials. Some of his fears had left him, too. He was in excellent humour. "Mister, if you think we can load that ferry like you have just told me, then let's try and load it. I think ten head will make us a load."

When Rawhide heard this, he jumped off the wagon pole and shouted, "Three cheers for our ferry operator. We'll try not to make much trouble for you. We'll all ride our best cutting horses for the job."

The man said, "Thanks for the coffee and big feed. If we don't have any trouble loading the ferry, we should have the whole works on the other side of the river before dark."

Little Bill was singing his favourite song, and Rawhide was whistling loudly, keeping time to the tune, as they rode out to change horses for the big job.

Whalebone shouted to them, "Bring in Nightmare for me and old Captain for Curly."

As the riders were saddling their horses near the chuck wagon, I said, "Everybody listen close. Remember, the ferry operator is captain of the boat. I'm surprised he gave us a chance to load the ferry at all. If we have ever been proud of our cowboying stunts, now's the time to show our stuff. That big fellow said ten horses, and I feel sure that may be a big load. We'll put a long rope on old Baldy, just like the last time we ferried. Then we'll have the ferry operator hide himself somewhere on the ferry with Baldy's rope. When I give the word, he can lead Baldy onto the ferry. We'll work the nine head carefully toward Baldy. Be sure not to let one break back after we've made our split. We'll push a load on right behind Baldy. We have to cut out nine horses, no more and no less. We'll have to work together and watch closely. Now, let's go. The ferry operator is waiting and ready to load. We may be here half the night if we don't move."

When the first load was on, the horses seemed afraid to move as the ferry jiggled on its cables. The horses whinnied and looked at their shadows in the deep water.

"Mirror Landing," I said. "It really is like looking at glass—it's terribly deep water. I'm glad I'm not swimming old Captain across this place. The ocean must be as deep as the devil with all these big rivers running into it every day of the year, with no outlet. Just listen to that water slap the side of this scow."

Little Bill remarked, "Big George didn't come with us this first trip. I wonder why. I guess he's getting trail weary. All he uses for a wagon seat is a hard board with a robe laid over it, but usually he's happy as long as he gets his three good meals a day. He sure is a tough man for his age."

"It's a long way across this river," shouted Rawhide above the whinnying horses and the noise of the water hitting the ferry.

Little Bill said, "I sure hope none of this bunch will try to swim back again. Old Cap would know that he was having a swim if he tried swimming across here with a tight cinch and the reins between his feet. I'm going to do some fishing in this river when we get finished. I'll have something more to tell my sister back home."

By about nine o'clock that night, the last load of horses trotted off the ferry and we waved goodbye and our thanks to the relieved operator. Then we set up camp among the thick trees on the north side of the river, where grazing was spotty but water was plentiful.

"It's a good thing we don't have to do this every day," sighed Big George, "or we'd be on the trail forever. I'm sure my wagon tires are getting thin. We've used up a tub of grease already, and my wagon could stand some more in the morning. This is wild-looking country through here. The ferry operator told me we'd pass some trappers' cabins before long, but there are not many people living between here and Slave Lake village. He also told me that muskegs would be our greatest dread. Grizzlies will be second, and mosquitoes, sand flies, flying ants, and deer flies will be next on the list.

"We should live off the grouse and wild berries from here on. I saw some lovely berry patches today, just ripe enough to eat. This country would be all right if it wasn't so thick with poplar and if it had a little grazing land. I'll get myself a crock when we reach Slave Lake."

A few days later, and through the same terrain, we were working our way westward. Occasionally we had to pull a horse or two from the muskeg. We took a thorough count each time we left a campsite. Little Bill would ride through the herd and take his count, then Rawhide would follow and take one. I always took a count as well.

"Counting horses in this brush is something like counting chickens," I told the riders, "so be careful. They always dodge in among one another, and it's easy to lose track." Any time the riders' totals did not tally, a re-count was made. If a horse was missing, it was likely to be in a muskeg, so we went searching for it.

There were times when we found plenty of feed in a wild grass meadow. Here, fallen logs had been decaying for a hundred years or more. We never passed by a place like this. I often saw where moose and deer bedded down in such places—there were many hoof marks where they had tramped around through the tall grass. In such places, the lads could see where moose had chewed off small new-growth trees for food. They looked as though they had been cut off with a sharp axe.

In many places the road was narrow. In other areas, a sixty-five-foot-wide path had been chopped out, with a trail in the centre. Quite often, the tree stumps stood on each side, to be pulled out later. Whenever the stumps were pulled and the sun was able to reach the ground, a grass called red top grew tall.

The Peace River Drag was a very crooked trail, bearing through the trees in a northwesterly direction. One day along this trail, we came to what looked like a clearing of a few acres. On second inspection, we found it to be all water with a graded road running straight through the centre. I was riding on the lead with the herd strung out behind me. Rawhide and Little Bill were bringing up the rear. When the horses walked out onto this narrow grade, they stopped to drink. More horses came onto it, and in no time the graded road was about ten inches below water. The horses moved along and sipped away, while I held my breath. I was afraid the horses would step off the grade and have to be pulled out.

When they were finished drinking, the horses quietly moved on. When this heavy weight was gone, the grade rose to the top of the water again. This must be what is called a corduroy road, I thought. It must have been built in the winter on the ice.

When the herd was well past this place, I let it move on while I waited for the boys, who were taking a good look at the muskeg. When the young riders came to meet me, I was singing my favourite song.

A cowboy's life is a happy one.
Some say it's free from care.

He sings as he rides from morning till night,
In the breeze on the prairie so bare.

"What are you so happy about?" Rawhide shouted. "I was almost petrified. I can hardly talk, let alone sing."

Little Bill grinned as he said, "That road looks as natural as ever. Somebody must have put a lot of rubber in that grade."

While we sat on our horses chatting about the muskeg we had just passed, Rawhide showered me with questions. "Do you think this road will take us close to the big hay meadows the Empress Mountie told us about? If they're as large as he told us, they'll be something to see. I wonder if it's all owned by someone. Do you suppose we could get a lease on a section or two? Maybe we could camp there and put up hay until the snow comes."

"We would certainly appreciate that kind of luck," I replied. "We'd buy ten new mowers, hire twenty-five Indians, and ship hay all over the drought area of southern Saskatchewan and Alberta. What a big business that would be. Every municipality down there will have to buy hay this year. We'll investigate that deal if we ever get to Slave Lake."

"Any idea how far we are from those hay meadows now?" Little Bill asked.

"If our luck holds out, and we don't bog too many horses in the muskeg, we should reach that settlement in a couple more days," I told him.

The Flying Dutchman
Lives Up
to His Name

<hr>

I N TWO DAYS, AS I HAD PREDICTED, WE WERE LOOKING across one of the largest hay meadows in Alberta, maybe the largest in western Canada. It was quite a thrill to see the roads graded high, and water seeping into the ditches. The hay resembled a farmer's corn crop for height and coarseness. Approaches were built in intervals along the ditches. When a horse or two would dodge across these crossings into the meadow, the tall grass reached the rider's saddle skirts. This was something for us prairie boys to see.

The hay meadow was on the east end of Lesser Slave Lake and must have covered a couple of townships or more. Along the roadside were numerous hummocks resembling large ant hills, as high as a man's knee. Here, young stock could almost lose themselves. On the south side of this graded road were many cleared areas covering several acres. In most of these clearings, tame hay had been planted and grew well. Other small fields held a few dairy cows of Holstein or Ayrshire breeding. Some of these fields were fenced with large tree roots, some were enclosed with barbed wire, and others with stake poles. We had never seen the likes of this before.

The young riders' dreams were coming true. They were only

about twelve miles from Lesser Slave Lake and the village of Slave Lake. Their spirits began to rise as they thought about the fishing they would do there. Their heads filled with images of the haystacks they would make if they were lucky enough to lease a piece of these meadows.

At noon, we stopped for dinner. After everything was cleaned up and ready for the road, Whalebone and I shoed two saddle horses.

"Boys, there's another horse that needs shoeing badly," said Little Bill. "She's a big Percheron mare, maybe ten years old. She's never been halter-broken. She used to be one of the wild bunch, but lately she's getting as ornery as the old devil. One of her hind feet has a deep, jagged split in the hoof. She's been limping a little for a few days, and it seems to be getting worse. For the last day or two, she's lagged behind the herd, and yesterday and today, she's tried to kick us off our saddle horses every time we try to hustle her along."

I finished shoeing my horse and said, "I'm sorry about that big grey mare being lame. I've been watching her, too. I'll bet she'll be as savage to shoe as a grizzly bear. She has shown me her teeth and tried to kick me, too. She must weigh fifteen hundred pounds. However, if she doesn't improve, some of these fellows who are forever trying to trade horses with us may get her in a trade. The first good camping place we find where we can stop over for a day, and when I get the nerve, I'll put a shoe on that split hoof."

Whalebone must have urged his long-legged horse on the lead to a fair pace because he rolled the covered wagon into the village of Slave Lake before sundown. The town was situated on higher ground than the hay meadow beside it. To the east and north, as far as the eye could see, were tall hay and haystacks. Beside the village, on the north and west, was Lesser Slave Lake. When we looked, all we could see was water. From this village to the west end of the lake was seventy-five miles, and they claimed it was thirty-five miles wide. No one ever told us exactly how many miles deep, but it was teeming with good-quality fish that were large enough to satisfy Little Bill and Rawhide.

When Whalebone entered the village, he asked the first man he met, "Where can I find a decent place to park my chuck wagon where there is grazing for a hundred horses for the night?"

The stranger replied, "There's some good grass patches south of town about a mile. Nothing should bother you there. You can park your wagons anywhere you like."

We stopped to graze the herd along the roadside. By the time we came along with the horses, Big George and Whalebone had camp set up, with the tent pitched right close to the cemetery. They were hustling to prepare supper.

"There's lots of room for the horses about a mile south of here," Whalebone said. "Better take a look to make sure. A man just told me there's plenty of grass out that way and that our stock couldn't hurt a thing."

Rawhide and I left Little Bill at the new camp and went on for about a mile with the horses. We rode around to examine the grazing prospects and found some of the oddest fences we had ever seen. Some fencing, about a quarter of a mile long, was made entirely of stump roots that were piled high. No animal larger than a small dog could crawl through. Other fences were made of poles. Instead of posts set in the ground for support, there were two shorter poles wired together in the form of a big X, with poles wired to them. A few other fences were strung tight with barbed wire. Most of the grass was red top.

We returned to camp just in time for a hot supper. Little Bill scolded the wagon men for setting up camp near a burying ground. We heard him say, "I'll be seeing tombstones in my dreams."

In less than a minute, Whalebone began to string off some spooky yarns about cemeteries. Little Bill put his hands over his ears, trying hard not to hear the cook's stories.

"We'll keep these two horses tied here tonight, in case of an emergency," I told the boys. "After midnight, I'll get up and ride circles for an hour or two. You fellows get a good sleep tonight. If the stock are in a quiet place, we can all sleep late in the morning. I've been doing with much less sleep that I ever did in my life. We have to catch up a little now and again."

When I had finished my night-herding job, turning back all stragglers, I was surprised to see how light it had become. The northern lights were dancing back and forth; I could almost see the brands on the horses.

As I settled myself into my bedroll, my responsibilities kept cropping up in my mind: If our chuck box is short of anything, we would be as well to fill it up here at this village. According to the map, there must be nearly a hundred miles of flag stations and Indian reserves galore along the lake. I'm not worried about water for the stock as long as we're near this lake, but I don't know what we'll do for grass. I'll try not to worry about it and tak'er as we find'er. The first thing I'll do in the morning is inquire about making hay on these meadows. We may be able to lease half a township, and, in that case, we would break every horse in the outfit on mowers like we used when I was a kid.

The next morning, town folks, old and young, were walking out to see the big herd of horses. I met some old prairie stockmen who were retired and living in Slave Lake. When these fellows heard of a large herd camping overnight, they became lonesome to see the horses and wanted to talk horse to the men in charge. By the time we were ready to catch the horses for the day, we found that the herd was quite nervous, owing to so many strangers trying to get close.

We all had trouble catching our horses. I wanted my grey gelding, the Flying Dutchman, as this was his day for the road. Oats in a can failed to impress them, so we had some rope practice. Some ropes were flying and missing. The Flying Dutchman threw his head to the ground and dodged, while skipping in and out through this big bunch of broncs. He was behaving like a wild duck instead of a saddle horse.

Rawhide grinned and said, "Curly, that grey is fixing to raise the devil with you this morning." He laughed again. "Providing that we can rope him. He's been awfully hard to catch lately. Last time we wanted him, I had quite a time. I had the rope set up among some trees, but when he saw it hung up there, he jumped plum over it and took off. The next time I brought him in, I had to lasso him. He seems stirred up for some reason this morning. Let's corner him against this pole fence."

When the grey gelding was led away from the other horses, he was so nervous he did not want me to place a hand on him. I unsaddled the horse I had ridden during the night and turned him loose into the bunch to graze his breakfast. The Flying Dutchman only snorted at the saddle lying on the ground.

An old gentleman with a wide moustache was standing close by, watching with interest. He spoke to me, saying, "Mister, you had better look out for that fellow this morning. He may have a lot of kinks to take out when you climb up on his top deck."

I picked up my saddle blanket with one hand, holding tightly onto my hackamore rope with the other. The horse snorted. I tried to hold the saddle blanket in front of him, hoping he would touch it with his nose and calm down a bit before I tried to saddle him. But the grey would have none of that this morning. He tried to run backwards and pull away.

Rawhide saddled his horse and watched me with my pony. He grinned a little as he came toward me and said, "Let me give you a hand."

I led my horse in a small circle for a minute or two. Finally I rubbed his neck and led him back toward the saddle where it lay on the ground, and picked up my blanket again. Quietly, I unfolded it over the horse's back. When I turned to reach for the saddle, the grey jumped, bucked, and whirled, throwing the saddle blanket into the dirt. Before I got straightened up, the horse jumped against me, still looking at the fallen blanket. Then he stepped onto one of my spurs and tripped me.

Rawhide roared with laughter and shouted, "I believe you picked a good name for the grey."

I limped around for a minute or two, gently cussing the horse in a very low voice, and commenced to saddle him in earnest. The old gentleman who was watching was not at all disappointed. It was beginning to look like the biggest rodeo the village of Slave Lake had ever seen.

Rawhide jumped his horse against mine and took a dally on the

Curly and his trick horse Diamond. *Courtesy Marlene Davidson*

saddle horn. He whispered, "This pony will need all his wind for the day's ride. There's no use breaking your legs among these trees, putting on a free show for this bunch of strangers."

"I'm already skinned up," I answered. "I hit my knee on some of those poplars, and for a second I thought that I broke my leg. When he stepped on my spur back there, he kind of sprained my weak ankle. I had that ankle broken about ten years ago, and it often gives me trouble."

I looked at the herd Little Bill had bunched. It was time to make a start. "Cowboy," I said, "we don't have a lot of time to sit here. Just jump your horse right into this grey and gallop off. I'm sure he'll follow you. He's mad at the world this morning, and he wants a holiday."

When we found the government agent and inquired about the hay meadow, we were told that all the good meadows had already been leased. The agent said, "I think you could buy all the haystacks you need, but their quality is not the best. If you fellows are travelling farther west, no doubt you'll be able to buy good oat sheaves, good hay, and plenty of straw when you reach Grande Prairie. If you want them, crops are excellent out that way this year. All the hay in these big meadows will be shipped out of here this winter. By the time the last of it is baled, it'll be frozen and poor."

It was a disappointment, but we knew there must be more good pasture farther along the trail. So, once again, we gathered the herd and were on our way.

The Crew
Is Left Horseless

W E HAD NOT MET A WAGON OR A CAR ON THE ROAD ALL forenoon. As we rode, we were talking, and wondering what the trail ahead would be like.

"We may have trouble finding grass," I said, "but as long as we follow Lesser Slave Lake, we should have plenty of water and fish. If we're lucky enough to find some grass patches through here, we won't want to pass them up. We'll have to keep these horses filled with something besides water. The first grass we find, we'll make camp and rest up again. We can do our washing and have a bath, a haircut, and a shave. Whalebone is a fair barber for a jack-of-all-trades guy like he is. He's a good ranch hand, a good horseshoer, and what he lacks in cooking skills is made up for by the quantity he feeds us."

The boys replied, "We're not grumbling any. We certainly don't want his job."

Two o'clock rolled around, and we still had no dinner. Whalebone was on the lead, watching for a grass patch big enough to feed the horses. When Whalebone and Big George saw an open spot of grass, each gave a war whoop and pulled their wagons off the road. They unhitched their horses from the wagons and turned them loose to graze, then laid the bridles beside the wagon and hustled to prepare some dinner.

We were hungry, as usual, and smiled when we came upon the small clearing, where we found Whalebone and Big George making dinner. We loosened the horses' cinches slightly and took off their bridles, then turned our ponies into the herd and made a bee line to the chuck wagon, where we washed for dinner.

Fires had burned through this area, and red top grew in abundance. The half-burned windfalls left behind were as dry as a bone, ready for lightning to strike again and start a new forest fire. Wild raspberries, ripe for picking, grew beside some of these old logs. Chipmunks and red squirrels chattered and scampered away, seeking to hide from us strangers. They were curious, too. They ran back and forth with their chirps and chatters, which may have been a warning to the crew to move on before trouble came to us.

When our stomachs were filled again, we pitched in to help Whalebone. We washed the dinner dishes, chopped dry wood from the nearby windfalls, and picked a few berries.

The horses spread over the clearing, filling themselves with grass and rolling as if they were enjoying themselves. Crusader, the Percheron stallion, was contentedly eating his oats while tied to Big George's wagon. The baby colt was nursing and frolicking about. She was happy to be loose with her mother. The horses scattered farther away from camp toward the lake, but no one could see them through the forest of trees.

Some of the boys were sitting on a log smoking and talking about our good luck in finding a camping spot big enough so we could rest for a day. Suddenly, a train whistle blasted. It seemed to be right beside us. The men bounded off the log in a hurry. We picked up our bridles and started looking for a pony to catch. None of us had noticed the railroad track beside us, hidden in the brush.

I shouted, "Our horses must all be on the tracks. Just listen to that engineer pull on his whistle. It sounds as if that train is rolling fast, and I can't even see one horse." We scrambled to find something to ride as the train whistle screeched.

Some horses that had been grazing along the open cut line by the tracks had started to run at the first whistle. The only clear path was down the railroad tracks to the west, away from the train. With the steam whistle blowing continually, the horses ran for their lives. The train seemed to be a short one, and the horses that were not ahead of the train got on the tracks and followed behind at a full gallop.

We ran through the brush toward the tracks as fast as we could. "There isn't a horse left," shouted Whalebone. "Only one big stud tied to the wagon. The saddle horses are all gone with their saddles, and all our harness horses are gone with their traces dragging. We'll never see them again."

Rawhide shouted from back in the brush, "Come over here, fellows, and help me. I found old Dick, but the crazy old cuss won't let me catch him."

It didn't take long for the five of us to surround old Dick and get a bridle on his head, but he was nervous.

An excited Little Bill exclaimed, "That's the last horse we have left."

Whalebone was cussing mildly. Big George looked upset as he said, "That train man was having a lot of fun at our expense."

My mind was in a whirl, too, as I tried to help Rawhide mount old Dick without a saddle. The young cowboy was in a hurry to get after the train and our horses. This made the horse even more excited. When Rawhide touched old Dick with his spurs to get him moving, the horse immediately bucked him off, headfirst, into the brush. Rawhide held a firm grip on the riding reins so the horse could not pull away from him. In another second or two, he was back for a reride. I helped him on again and could soon hear them galloping along the railroad tracks as if the train was after them, too. He looked like John Gilpin as he rode up the tracks.

Every one of us felt bad about being left this way.

"No use worrying," I said. "Rawhide is after them now, and if that train didn't run over them, or push them into the lake, he'll bring them back. He'll likely be blistered from the hot horse sweat, since he's without a saddle, but he'll get them. He's a better man riding bareback than some of our best cowpokes with a two-hundred-dollar saddle. Let's go back, drink some coffee, and quit worrying about a runaway horse or two."

Little Bill complained, "Losing a hundred horses is not exactly peanuts."

We returned to camp and drank more coffee, but we were a silent bunch. We looked at Crusader tied to the wagon. Big George said, "A ton of horse flesh, but he wasn't built for speed. Who knows, we may all have to ride him out of here."

Just at that moment, Little Bill roared, "Look, boys, here's another horse. He picked up his oat can and hustled toward the horse as it came walking out of the brush. It was a big harness mare that belonged to Big George.

Little Bill looked at the horse for a minute and said, "We have this mare and the stud now, so we'll all be able to ride in the wagon if we don't find the big bunch."

Whalebone said, "My new saddle is still rolled up in a tarp in my wagon. Why doesn't somebody think of these things instead of sending that boy off after those horses riding bareback? I sure wish I had a horse to put it on."

About an hour later, another train came from the west, whistling at each whistle post. It passed the empty horse camp.

Big George exclaimed, "What will become of Rawhide now, Curly? Do you suppose that's the same train coming back after leaving us all on foot away out here among the grizzlies, cougars, and wild cats?"

Little Bill was concerned about his friend. "We won't see Rawhide again today after that second train. I sure wish I had a good horse to ride."

Meanwhile, the horses ahead of the train had gone about three miles before they saw an opening toward the lake and left the tracks. The horses running behind the train caught up to the leaders, and Rawhide found about sixty of them between the tracks and the lake, on the north side. On the south side, the balance of the herd had found the cut line of the Peace River Drag where it ran close to the tracks. They were heading west at a fair pace when Rawhide took after them.

The afternoon was hot and sultry. Sweat ran down the horses' legs to their feet. Their earlier fright left them in a nervous state.

Somehow Rawhide managed to get ahead of the horses and tried to get a count. He was doing a lot of figuring in his head as he gathered this bunch and brought them all together. He tried hard to catch a horse that was carrying a saddle, but was unable to do so. When he was satisfied with his count, he started back toward the camp, feeling very pleased with himself.

Rawhide was following the herd down the railroad tracks, trying to take them slowly, when he saw a man working on the tracks. Before the cowboy had a chance to say hello, the man shouted, "Get those horses off the tracks! There's another train due here in less than ten minutes."

Once more, Rawhide put old Dick into high gear and tried to push the herd off into the brush toward the cut line of the trail. They all raced madly down the side of the tracks. The horses put on an extra burst of speed, and a wagon horse ran in front of Rawhide, dragging a trace chain that hooked on a railroad spike. The harness strap broke, and the horse galloped on, leaving a full set of heavy harness on the tracks. The train whistled less than half a minute away. Rawhide hesitated long enough to scoop up the harness and then galloped on. He had just turned the last horse from the tracks and had barely cleared them himself when the train went whistling by.

"Of all the countries in the world for a cowboy, this is the worst I can think of," Rawhide said aloud. "What business do two trains have in this wilderness when I have horses running crazy on their tracks?"

While the crew watched from farther up the railroad tracks, Rawhide calmly drove the herd into camp along the Peace River Drag. Everybody started to cheer as a whistling Rawhide turned the herd into the clearing.

Little Bill shouted, yodelled, and sang one of his cowboy songs, which seemed good enough proof that he was happy again. He caught his roan mare and tried to brush the caked sweat from her hide and hair, then looked her over thoroughly for cuts and scratches.

Rawhide explained to the crew just how he had managed to get around the herd and how the second train had run them off the tracks. "I feel sure that we'll be in far more trouble later. This road is hardly ever more than a quarter of a mile away from the tracks, and sometimes it's only a few rods away. We'll never know when we're close to a train until we hear its whistle. What do you say about camping in this spot now? That train is likely to come through here again."

I replied, "We'll move camp right away. I'd rather night herd in the brush than go through this again. We'll move up the road, and when Whalebone sets up camp for the night, we'll be ready to call it a day."

Shoeing
a Bronco Mare,
and Disaster

....

ABOUT THREE DAYS LATER, WE FOUND A FAIR-SIZED
clearing within sight of the lake. The railway was close to the
lake shore, and the large buildings of a fish hatchery were situated
on the shore line. There was some grass in this clearing, and the
horses had a good fill.

"After supper, I'll take the herd back about a mile to a wide place
on the cut line," I told the boys. "There's enough grass for tonight
since they're filled up. I'll night herd them out there. You fellows
can swim and fish as long as you like. I saw fish two feet long out
there, jumping out of the water after flies. If you can't catch them
with your hook, you can lasso them."

That evening when the horses were gathered, there was one
horse missing from the count. After a thorough check, we discovered it was Little Bill's roan mare.

The young riders were excited, and Little Bill said, "If someone
has taken her, I'll hunt the whole countryside until I find her. I'll
never own another horse like her."

We began to search the surrounding area. I followed the shore
of the lake, another man hunted back over the cut line, while the
others looked for muskeg.

Along the lake shore was a deep, V-shaped ditch that drained from the railway to the lake. I followed the ditch and found the roan mare entirely helpless in the six-foot-deep ditch. It looked as if she had tried to jump over it and had fallen in. Her back was below the level of the ground, but her feet did not touch bottom, and her sides were tightly wedged. Luckily, the ditch was dry.

It didn't take me long to report to the crew. I hustled back to the wagon and began to unload the corral ropes to make a rope harness.

"Catch your gentle team, your muskeg pullers, and bring your eveners, too. Big George, bring a sharp axe so we can cut some poles to put underneath her."

It didn't take long to lift the roan out of the hole. The team took a good pull and raised her slightly, and the boys pushed the poles beneath her until she was on top of the ground. To our surprise, she was unhurt.

Little Bill whistled with joy and rubbed the horse's neck and back as if she were an infant. Big George said, "You can never tell what's behind a tree or a hill. It's either a ditch, a muskeg, or a train. The fellow who made this ditch didn't know he was setting a trap for one of the best ponies in northern Alberta."

A day or two after the mare was taken out of the ditch, there was more trouble. The black dog decided to sniff at a porcupine that sat huddled along the trail. Without warning, a swish of the porcupine's tail filled the dog's nose with quills. The dog cried, rolled, and pawed at his face. The poor fellow was in incredible pain, and Big George was desperate to help him. He waved at Whalebone to stop his wagon and wait. The two men soon removed dozens of quills. Each time a quill was pulled, it was followed by blood and a sharp whine from the dog.

When camp was made later in the day, we all took a turn pulling quills. The black dog had a sore nose for some time. We were not sure if Big George felt worse about his horse in the muskeg or quills in his dog's nose.

The big grey mare with the split hoof had been lagging behind for a week or more and becoming more ornery each day. She would lay back her ears and show her teeth at the riders, and if a fellow rode too close, he was sure to be kicked. The long run ahead of the train did not help her sore foot or her disposition.

"We'll try to put a horseshoe on that foot at noon today if we ever catch the wagon," I told the boys. "She sure is holding us up lately."

We debated whether the mare would follow us if we left her behind the herd. We decided to try, then watched to see what she did. She nibbled at the sparse grass as we went about three miles down the trail, where we found that Whalebone had set up camp and made dinner.

After dinner, I exclaimed, "We may as well stop here until tomorrow. We can put plates on the front feet of the saddle horses who need them. When the grey mare comes in, we'll shoe her, too. Any of you boys carry life insurance?"

Whalebone answered, "There is no insurance for a horse wrangler or a rodeo man, unless he pays more than he can earn."

Soon Big George, Whalebone, and I were very busy shoeing. When the grey mare did not arrive, the two boys tossed a coin to see who would go back for her. It was Little Bill's misfortune to lose, so he saddled a fresh horse and rode back to bring her in. When he found her, he noticed that she had not moved any closer to the herd. She was rested now and willing to travel at a slow walk.

This young cowboy was of a happy nature. He was singing, whistling, and enjoying the scenery along the trail. The mare was limping and travelling very slowly. Little Bill followed her up the trail while he watched the little cottontail rabbits, chipmunks, and different kinds of squirrels. He got off his horse and picked what ripe berries he could find and soon caught up with the grey mare. He walked behind her, leading his pony, and would occasionally flick the mare with the end of his riding reins to hustle her along.

But when Little Bill was looking the other way, she kicked at him with both feet. In a flash, he saw what was happening and ducked sideways. She missed him with one foot, but the other foot nearly hit his face, banging the side of his head. It cut a deep slash through his hair and scalp, and Little Bill fell into a heap on the side of the road.

When he finally came to, the cowboy felt sleepy. He put his hand to his head and found that he was bleeding. He roused himself and saw the mare close by. He felt sleepy again, but knew he'd better get moving. He wondered how much blood he could safely lose and still make it back to camp.

Little Bill did not feel like singing now. He felt dizzy as he tried to mount his saddle horse. He knew that the crew was busy at camp and would not come looking for him before evening. He also knew that no one was likely to come along this trail, so he took a firm grip on the reins and saddle horn and rode the three miles back to camp. All the while, he was afraid he might faint and fall off.

None of us saw Little Bill until he was among us. I looked up and gasped, "Holy cow, man, what happened to you? I'll bet it was a bear."

"No, it's not that bad," sighed Little Bill. "The old mare tried to kick me in the face. I guess it's only a scratch, but it's numb. I think it has bled quite a lot. I can't see it, but I sure felt it."

I dropped my shoeing hammer and led Little Bill's horse toward the chuck wagon. When I examined the wound and washed away some clotted blood from his ear, I knew this was a case for a doctor. A thick strip of hide with a patch of hair attached to it was loose and needed to be stitched back into place.

Little Bill repeated, "It doesn't hurt much now. It's kind of numb, and I feel just a tingle. We're so far from civilization out here. There's no doctor within a hundred miles. You go ahead and stitch me up if you think it needs it."

I replied, "Why, man, I could sew a cow all the way up her belly if I had to, but I don't have enough nerve for this unless it's real necessary. I have some court plasters somewhere in a kit in the cupboard. Maybe we can fix it with that."

I carried a bed roll out into the shade of the wagon and had Little Bill lay down and rest while I found the first-aid kit. I came back carrying a can of turpentine, some iodine, a pair of scissors, and some court plasters. Then I clipped off some hair around the scalp wound.

"This won't hurt you, cowboy," I said. "It's the best thing I have to stop bleeding and ease pain. I always use it for stock and on myself, too."

When I poured on the turpentine, I felt Little Bill flinch. I picked up the iodine bottle and whispered, "This stuff will hurt like hell for about a minute, but after that first sting is over, you should feel good very quickly. It always helps me. I should carry a barrel of iodine with me—I'm forever getting skinned up."

When I poured the iodine into the wound, Little Bill jumped off the bed roll and cussed, hopping around as if he had stepped on a bee's nest. I waited about a minute until the pain stopped and I thought it was safe to go near him again.

"That big flap of hide hanging down could be sewn back up with ten stitches or more. I'll plaster it together with these court plasters. You'll have to lie on that bed roll all afternoon and be still. Who knows, maybe tomorrow as well. If you run much of a fever by evening, we'll pick our best horse and light out of here for a doctor. I'll watch you close. I want you to relax. Don't worry about anything."

The next morning Little Bill was much better. His temperature was down, and he declared that he was able to ride. He looked very odd wearing a light bandage around his head that covered one ear and tied under his chin. His cowboy hat sat at a jaunty angle. We heard him singing about riding the range of glory on an old cow horse.

The grey mare did not come to camp. Whalebone and I decided that we would handle her and shoe her wherever we found her. We put some tools and horseshoes together in a sack and rode out on the back trail to meet the mare. We found her where Little Bill had left her. When we rode close, the mare showed her teeth, wheeled, and kicked. We had no time to fool around, but we did not want to be kicked or bitten.

Whalebone built a loop in his lariat and necked her. This was the only rope she had ever had on her since she was branded about nine years earlier. While she was rearing around, I roped her front feet, and the two saddle horses took her to the ground with a bump and a bang. We tied three of her feet together and went to work on her.

The split hoof had a stone in it about the size of a large bird's egg. It was wedged in so deeply and had been there so long that the frog of her foot was festering badly. We dug the stone out first and examined her other feet for stones and gravel, then trimmed all her jagged hooves and nailed a plate on the sore one. I poured some turpentine into the festered frog and untied her feet to let her up.

The mare whinnied a few times and then limped up the trail. We gathered up our tools and tied them back on our saddles. When we caught up to the mare, she seemed to be walking much better.

"Curly," said Whalebone, "I was expecting much more trouble than we had. I brought along my Luger, and if that old cuss tried to get one of us down, I would have plunked her between the eyes. The wolves and bears would have had a feed. She'll be all right in a day or two. There's lots of fight left in her. She sure gave Little Bill a heck of a crack. If he hadn't ducked his head when he did, we'd be burying him tomorrow."

When we returned to camp and put away our saddle horses, Whalebone noticed that I was limping. "Now what's the matter with you? Is your riding boot pinching your foot?"

"Oh no, the Flying Dutchman stepped on my spur and turned my old broken ankle. I also banged my knee against a tree that same day, and it seems to hurt more than my ankle."

"When I get married," said Whalebone, "I'm going to quit handling broncs. It's too dangerous, and a fellow will get rheumatism when he gets old from the broken bones he's sure to get."

"What will you do for excitement then?" I asked.

"I think I'd like to be a big-game hunter."

"Lord love us, and you say this is dangerous! You better stick to broncs and rheumatism if you want a longer life."

"Why do you say that?"

"Well, first thing, you're a prairie man. You have no experience with animals larger than skunk, porcupine, badger, or coyote. I hear these grizzly bears are very ferocious animals. Your Luger would be no better than a pop gun if we were attacked. A bear was close to our camp this morning, and he smelled as strong as an old pig pen. I saw where he tore a rotten log apart and ate the ants. I hope he got enough of them for his breakfast and doesn't want to top it off with one of our saddle horses, or bacon from our chuck box."

Whalebone gave a whistle and said, "We must be in grizzly bear country, all right. I've smelled something like that for over a week, but I thought it was some bad weeds."

I replied, "My map shows this to be grizzly bear country from Athabaska to the Rocky Mountains. We'd better keep shells handy for our rifles. If they don't bother me, I sure won't bother them. This is their country, and I say, let them have it."

Whalebone had other ideas. "I'd sure like to have the hide off a big one for my floor when I build my log cabin."

"I saw a bear track in the mud this morning that was bigger than Big George's foot," I told him. "Three nights ago, a bear came so close when I was night herding on an open cut line that my horses all pulled out. I didn't tell the boys, but that's the reason I'm taking a look at the herd every night. I'm packing my forty-four, too."

Swimming
the Little Smoky

N EARLY EVERY DAY, WHALEBONE HAD AN INDIAN LAD OR two riding with him in the chuck wagon. Whenever the cook needed fresh fish, the boy would go quietly to the shore of the lake with a fishing line, walk out on a big log in the water, and always return with two fish.

One day Whalebone asked one of the youngsters, "Why don't you bring enough for breakfast, too?"

The lad answered, "Oh no, I'll catch some in the morning." He would never catch more than would be eaten at one meal. It was his belief that no fish should be wasted.

Once our outfit moved away from the lake area, we found a number of settlements. Indians spent many evenings at our night camps—some wanted to sell fish, some wanted to hear Little Bill sing, and others wanted to trade their cowboy trinkets.

One evening I said, "You boys will have to tie all your new horses to a tree or some place. I'll be glad when you quit trading horses. We have more trouble with those horses than all the rest of the herd. I've ridden forty extra miles to get them back."

Rawhide replied, "I'm night herding tonight, and if those new horses give that much trouble, we'll trade them off again."

Roads were good around High Prairie, and we were glad to be out of the woods where we could see the country. Provisions for the chuck wagon were bought at High Prairie. Some farmers wanted to buy a few teams of horses. The horses were cheap, but the farmers could not obtain credit at a bank so no sales were made.

The time came for us to decide if we should follow the loop going north, toward the town of Peace River. We talked to local people about the roads going west and were told that no road went very far in that direction. To go north, around the big loop, meant crossing the Peace River at Peace River town. We would also have to cross a railroad truss with no sides. The Peace River made a big loop, and the road crossed it again at Dunvegan, where there was a ferry. We were told that the Alberta government was making a cut line from the Big Smoky River through to the Sturgeon Lake country and joining up with High Prairie.

I asked about the bridges and ferries on this proposed road between High Prairie and Grande Prairie and learned there was one ferry somewhere on the Big Smoky, but there were no ferries or bridges on the Little Smoky River. If we followed the cut line, we would avoid crossing the Peace River twice. The horses had a fair rest and fill while we debated the best route to take.

An old trapper visited the wagon and ate dinner with us. He was acquainted with the woods to the southwest toward the Smokys.

"There's an Indian trail running out that way," he said. "The trail is narrow and crooked. The wooden culverts, made of small poles, are old and rotten, but the Indians still use the trail. They swim the Little Smoky when the water is low. Wherever they've made a cut line, the stumps are still standing, and men are working out that way, pulling stumps with big cats. You would save yourself 150 miles of travel if you can get through that jungle of forest."

We considered this matter seriously. I said, "Look here, fellows, the Peace River is in the neighbourhood of six hundred yards wide. Do you remember how far that is? Our biggest rifle would shoot only halfway across there. The railroad truss is entirely out of the question. It reminds me of the road crossing the muskeg. It's too far to swim. The trapper says the Indians can cross the Little Smoky with a buckboard when the water is low. The Big Smoky has a ferry. What do you fellows think about the adventures ahead?"

The lads shouted, "Across we go!"

"British Columbia or bust," added Whalebone.

"We will be bust, too, if we can't sell some horses for cash," I remarked.

The northern lights shone each night, providing many hours of daylight. The outfit left High Prairie in a southwesterly direction. When we had left civilization behind, we found the Indian trail and followed it. It was impossible to make very good mileage. The poplar trees were as thick as they could grow. The first day on this narrow trail, the herd came up against a road block. A wagon with a wide flat bottom, loaded with oil barrels, was covering the full width of the trail. It had a broken axle, and whoever was in charge had left it there. We had to chop out a bypass to take the horses and wagons past. Not long after this axe work, Big George and Whalebone were obliged to cut down a number of poplar poles and retop a small pole bridge to get their wagons across. We had new experiences every day.

We did not find many grass patches for the stock along this route. Late one Saturday evening, we came to the banks of the Little Smoky River.

"Big timber must have covered all of this country at one time," said Big George. "Those dry old windfalls look to be 150 feet long. Trees have burned and over time have grown up again."

"It looks like hell to me," I answered. "I can't see an armful of grass anywhere. We're all half-starved for our supper, and here we are up against this big river. This place will have to be the end of our trail for today, regardless of how it looks."

"This trail led us to a rapids on the river," said Big George. "Do you suppose this is where the Indians cross? The foam is a foot deep along the shore, and just listen to the roar of the water."

"I bet the Indians just cross here in the winter when it's frozen," I answered. "I haven't seen a fresh track of a buckboard anywhere. Do you see that big sandbar out in the middle? I wonder if that would carry a fellow, or would he go down out of sight like he was in muskeg?"

"This looks like a bad place to hunt for horses," Rawhide said.

"They'll cover a couple of sections before morning, hunting for peavine. I don't see anything else for them to eat around here."

"We'll have to wait for daylight to cross this river," I replied. "I'm worried about how we'll manage it. Tomorrow, I'll try to swim old Captain across. If he has trouble, I'll turn back and make a raft of some kind for the wagons, or we may have to turn back to some other route."

Some time Sunday morning, a few saddle horses were brought to the wagon. I caught my faithful pony, Captain, and saddled him. It seemed as if everyone in the crew was looking down their nose at my attempt to cross these rapids.

The roar of the river was so great that you would have to shout to be heard. Numerous large boulders, five or six feet high, lay below the surface, water whirling and foaming around their tops.

I mounted Captain and was ready to try my luck crossing the river when Rawhide galloped up beside me and said, "I'm riding Jack. He's my best saddle horse, and I'm going across that river with you. If I go under, you can take me out. If you go under, I'll take you out. What do you say, partner?"

We let our ponies take a drink of this cold mountain water and then gently urged them into the deep stream. On this side of the river, the current was swifter, and the ponies seemed to drift with it. But they managed to swim through the worst and touch bottom in some places. We swam and waded until we reached the big sandbar. It was solid and held us well. We rested our horses, and I got down from my saddle to look for buckboard tracks, hoping to find the best place to enter the river once more.

"I wonder if we can go straight across from here and find a place to get our ponies out." I said.

The saddle horses swam and waded as before and found a fair place on the opposite bank to climb out of the river. Here we dismounted and let the horses take a breather while we looked around for more wheel tracks and the Indian trail. When we climbed to the heights above the river, we found the trail. We also discovered a large tent set up among the poplar trees.

Rawhide looked at me. "We're not the only crazy campers in this wilderness. I wonder where they're going. Let's find out."

We led our horses among the trees toward the tent. There we found a dozen men passing the Sunday as best they could in their camp in the midst of the bush. Some of these working men were trying to sleep, but most of them were playing poker.

The foreman for these woodsmen asked, "Did you fellows drop out of an airplane somewhere? How in the world did you get here?"

"We were camped across the river all night with a large horse herd," I told him. "We're just out exploring to see if it's safe to bring our wagons over."

"We're a construction crew," said the foreman. "We've been working in this neck of the woods all summer. You fellows are the first white men we have seen. Where in this wilderness are you trying to go? There are no homesteads available through this part of the country yet, but no doubt it won't be long once this road gets finished. They claim this soil is suitable for agriculture clear across to Sturgeon Lake.

"I'll have some of our boys watch for you when you get ready to cross. There are a lot of boulders in that river—you don't want to straddle one with your wagon gear. Are you fellows strong swimmers in case a horse quits with you halfway across?"

"We're trusting our lives to these two ponies," I told him. "Neither one of us could swim across a water trough eight feet long."

Whalebone and Little Bill were standing along the river watching our swimming horses as we returned to camp. They were talking loudly, so their voices could be heard over the sound of the running water.

"Those riders look like little boys on a merry-go-round," shouted Little Bill. "I'm not sure I have a horse that can swim that far and carry me. I never rode a swimming horse in my life. Is it fun, Whalebone?"

Whalebone, at once, began to lay out a few important rules. "You have to give your horse a fairly slack cinch, sit straight, and be very still. If you rock sideways at all, you'll turn your horse over in the water. He'll be similar to a canoe and will turn upside-down just as easy. Be sure to sit still and give your horse his head. Don't bother him at all. Remember, he's swimming for his own life, too. Some horses will swim very low in the water with just the end of their nose above. But don't get excited and jump off. A swimming horse will climb on top of anything to get himself out of the water. In case you're put afloat by some accident, be sure to roll off behind your horse and get a good hold of his tail. Hang on and be careful not to swallow a lot of water. No matter what else happens, you can kick and paddle with one hand. Your horse will drag you along so you'll float, and he can't climb onto you."

When Rawhide and I got back to camp, we unsaddled our ponies and laid their saddles on the ground to dry. Our horses rested in the sun.

Little Bill was excited because Rawhide had made that swim ahead of him. He was very proud of his pal and fired questions at him about the adventure.

"Rawhide, I don't want to drown my roan mare. She's too small to pack me that far. What will I ride?"

"You can ride this horse of mine," Rawhide replied. "I know he can do it all right. I'll take old Dick. I'm not scared of that bronc now."

Whalebone and Big George also had their share of questions. I replied, "Boys, be sure to chain your wagon boxes solid to your wagon gear. The water is deep and swift. There are several big boulders in there, mostly on this side of the river. They're big solid rocks, and we'll have to travel among them. The water is swift and deeper on this side. If a box isn't well fastened, it'll float off the wagon, and where you'd go for a boat ride would be anybody's guess. The river is the most treacherous between here and the sandbar. If a wagon was to hang up on a big rock, it would be disastrous. I'll put my catch rope on one of your lead horses, and Rawhide will put his rope on the other. We'll take one wagon at a time. We'll be able to see the rocks and pilot you among them. A fellow can't tell where he is from a wagon. There won't be much to it if we all work together. Be very careful. We'd better take the herd of horses over first because we may need everybody's help to put them into the river."

It was noon by the time we had gathered the horses from the woods. One horse was missing so Little Bill held the herd close to the river while Rawhide and I went looking for it.

It was not long before I heard Rawhide shouting. The echo of his voice bounced around in all directions.

"I found her, Curly," he yelled. "Come and see where she was hiding."

When I got through the brush, I was surprised to see a black mare of good size with one back leg over a large tree limb.

"She must have tried to jump over that old tree," I said. "It looks like it's been a windfall for half a century. She was lucky not to have both hind legs over it. Maybe she's been there all night. How are we going to get her out?"

We tried to lift the mare's leg high enough to free her, but it was impossible. When we tried to help her, she snorted and plunged harder than ever. The inside of her leg was skinned and bleeding, but she still jumped.

"You stay with her," I told Rawhide, "and I'll go back to the chuck wagon for an axe. How did you happen to find her?"

"She heard my horse and whinnied to it. I would have gone right on by if she hadn't."

When we released the mare and chased her in with the herd, dinner was waiting.

"If we get into any trouble," said Whalebone, "I can always swim better with a full belly. A guy can't do much when he's hungry. The Lord only knows where we'll find a clear spot big enough to set up our next camp. If our groceries all get wet crossing the river, we won't have to dry them out for dinner today. Come, fellows, roll your spurs. I want everything packed and ready before you take the herd across."

When dinner was finished, Little Bill shouted to Whalebone, "Be sure to put my guitar in the top cupboard so it won't get wet. That old wagon will be full of water before you get to the sandbar. We won't have any dry clothes to change into and our riding boots will be full of water, too."

When we chased the herd into the fast-running river, the horses started swimming immediately. They whinnied wildly and swam their best. The colts and yearlings drifted slightly downriver and swam in a large circle toward the island of sand. Then they rested on the island, and the colts mothered up once more.

After the horses had rested a few minutes, I began to look toward the opposite shore to see if anyone from the construction gang was marking our landing place. I couldn't see anyone. We chased the herd into the river again, hoping we were guiding them toward the proper landing. Without too much trouble, the horses climbed out and ran up the steep hill toward the Indian trail.

Little Bill stayed to watch the horses while Rawhide and I returned to the old camp to guide the wagons across. Old Dick and Captain were good swimming horses, and they got plenty of practice this Sunday afternoon.

Whalebone had his four horses hitched and waiting. Big George was still harnessing his team, and I noticed that he had a fat balky mare that had not yet been hitched on our journey. I was surprised to see the big fellow with a horse he could not depend on.

"Why did you do such a thing?" I asked. "You'd have been better with a good honest pair until you got across."

Big George gave the mare an affectionate pat on the neck and said, "Oh, she'll be fine, Curly."

"It's your horse and your wagon, but I don't want to lose you two. You stay here while we take the chuck wagon across. We'll come back, put our ropes on your team, and guide you across, too," I told him.

The chuck wagon pushed the pole team quite hard while going down the steep grade into the river. Whalebone did not have to drive his team. Soon they were all into the river with the chuck wagon floating downstream toward the Big Smoky. The box bobbed up and down as much as the chains would allow. Whalebone was chewing tobacco and smiling as his lead team gained footing on the bottom. Some horses were wading while others were swimming. The whole outfit went along fairly well. Big George watched closely. From where he was sitting it looked quite easy.

The horses had a breather on the sandbar, and then the wagon was pulled into the river once again. It quickly floated sideways in the current. We led the team, trying to hurry, but we made sure that each move was safe. Hardly a word was spoken, as this was a new experience for all. The water in this river had its source somewhere in the mountains and was nearly as cold as ice. We reached the far side of the river safely and were just pulling the wagon out of the water when we heard a man's loud call for help.

We pulled the wagon to the top of the hill and looked to see who was shouting. It sounded more like an echo. We looked toward the far side of the river for Big George's wagon. It wasn't there. Once again, we heard a shout, "Curly!"

Our eyes searched the river, and we were horrified to see a wagon box among the boulders on the rapid side of the river. We heard Big George's voice again, "Curly!"

One of the boys said, "The big boy is hung up on a boulder. Maybe he has drowned his team."

"That dang old rascal," I said. "I told him to stay put and we would come and get him. Now we have real trouble. He's in the rapids in six or seven feet of water. I can't swim a bit. I'll have to take Whalebone's lead team back there with a set of eveners and a logging chain. Boys, I sure hate this job like hell, but I can't let the old fellow die from fright. I better get moving. I guess he's too old to take orders from a kid like me."

It is hard to describe how I got back across that river with a whiffletree, chains, and a team of horses. I had the team hitched to the eveners, with a clevis fastening one end of the chain to the eveners, and the other end hooked over my saddle horn. This big set of eveners, floating deep in the water to one side, as far as the chain would allow, made things confusing. I was sure my harness traces were under my horses' bellies. I was wondering how I would ever straighten them out again and was relieved to land on the sandbar and find that my team was not over the traces.

Big George continued shouting "Curly!" as loud as he could. The echo of his voice rang up and down the valley. I was getting to him as quickly as I could.

When I reached Big George he was still shouting, but I could scarcely hear what he was saying. His balky mare was standing on the river bottom with her head held high. The wagon had swung sideways and was braced against a boulder. The wagon box was jumping up and down as far as the chain would allow, while white foam whirled around it. If he had been driving any other horse in his string, he would never have gotten into this trouble, I thought. It looked as if his team was over its traces.

The current floated the eveners, keeping the chain so tight that I couldn't make it reach. Finally, I placed the team in such a position that my chain would make it there. I wanted Big George to hold tight to his wagon box and try to stand on the wagon pole in the water and hook the chain to the wagon. But when the big boy tried, the current swept his feet downstream in a hurry, and he couldn't do it.

Old Captain was braced against that current with white foam swirling over his back. I felt about as cold as in winter. I fumbled and dropped my team's driving reins. In a jiffy, they were out of my reach. I worked away and finally got the chain hooked. I nudged old Captain to where I wanted him and was able to recover my lines.

I took another look at Big George in the wagon, with water up to his knees. I had my mind made up that if that balky mare wouldn't walk, I would pull the wagon over top of her, harness and all.

I started the lead team and was surprised to see the mare was ready to go, too. We waded and swam until we reached the sandbar, where we rested ourselves and the horses.

Big George and I were both relieved when we pulled that wagon out of the river and placed it near the chuck wagon. We poured the water out of our boots and changed into some dry clothes. I had been doing some serious thinking while trusting my life to my faithful pony.

I told the boys, "A person who has never been sad is seldom, if ever, happy. I never felt sadder since we left home than I felt today. I certainly hated to take that lead team, swim them over that river, and hitch them to the wagon in the most treacherous part of the stream—no amount of money could have convinced me to do it. But now I'm happy because it's all over. I got a little water in my pockets and boots. I'm soaked, chilled, and near waterlogged, but am I ever glad we're across that place. I'll never cross there again until the Alberta government builds a bridge. By the time that happens, I may be too old to travel."

Big George was in as good a mood as the crew had ever seen him. He was telling jokes and laughing loudly, mostly due to his nerves.

"I thought for a while that Curly wouldn't come back for me. I should have done like he told me and stayed there, but it looked like a lot of extra work for him to come back. If I could've climbed out of that wagon and got back to shore, I sure would have. That current was so strong that if I had tried getting out, I would have landed up in the Peace River. My nerves are slipping."

I laughed with Big George, trying to make a joke of the whole affair. I said, "Don't lose your nerve, big boy. We'll need all the nerves that are left among us before we see another town. Maybe we can get you a little tonic at Grande Prairie. What do you say?"

The big fellow answered, "Curly, I have never needed a crock more in my life than I do right now, just for a nerve builder."

Big George
Gets Tired
of the Trail

A NUMBER OF MEN FROM THE CONSTRUCTION CREW TALKED with Little Bill and admired the horses that were washed so nice and clean from their swim across the river. One fellow wanted to make a deal with me for one of my horses. Little Bill walked toward the chuck wagon calling, "Curly, come over here for a minute. These men want to buy some horses. You'd better come and make a deal. They want to buy Pinto."

When I walked to where Little Bill was standing, I whispered, "These poker players have real cash. Whalebone declares that Pinto is not for sale—that he has first choice. I know that fellow is stuck on Pinto, and he won't buy any other."

The horse buyers had cash, but they were hard bargainers. Forty-five dollars was all I could get for the pinto gelding. Whalebone sold a matched team of unbroken bronc mares, Rawhide sold an unbroken horse, and Little Bill sold two. According to the deal, each animal had to have a halter on, and the men requested that we leave the horses tied to a tree. But there was no place to corral the horses and wrestle with them to put on their halters.

I talked to the fellow who bought Pinto and asked, "What'll you do with a horse in these woods? That horse has been halter-broken and is smart to learn, but he's a fairly wild cuss."

The new owner answered, "We'll get along fine. My dad calls me Cayuse Bill. I've been raised with that kind of horse in southern Alberta, so Pinto will suit me perfectly. You just tie him to a tree if you can, and I'll do the rest."

My saddle was on Captain, my favourite roping, swimming, and pick-up horse. We were all getting ready to tie a bronc to a tree, and I was going to try nabbing Pinto. My rope was soaking wet, and I knew if I made a mistake throwing it, I might as well say goodbye to Pinto. He wouldn't give me a second chance.

I rode around a bunch of perhaps twenty head, the spotted horse among them, and drove them to the shore line. There I tossed a loop over a snag and stretched the rope. Now I was ready for a crack at Pinto. When I turned the bunch back up the hill, Pinto was near the back of the group. I sat high in my stirrups and threw my wet lariat. The loop settled around Pinto's neck with a swish and dropped back near his shoulders. I took a dally on my saddle horn while Captain squatted down for the jerk. But the feel of the lariat made Pinto sprint for his life, and my catch rope broke where it was dallied around the saddle horn.

I'll never forget the performance that bronc put on as he ran through the bush with a rope between his legs. The horse snorted and buck-jumped like a mule in a circus. The construction crew laughed and cheered at the unexpected entertainment.

It was useless to follow the frightened horse until he settled down, so I rode back to where Cayuse Bill and his friends were watching. They were laughing and kidding the new owner about his spotted horse.

"Gentlemen," I said, "if you fellows will form a circle here, I'll bring Pinto back with five or six other horses. He's well halter-broken and is trailing twenty feet of rope. When I bring the horses into your circle, close in quickly. Whoever can catch the rope, give it a quick pull."

Pinto was nearly bucked out when I got around him and a few other horses. I brought them into the circle of men, who closed in fast. Cayuse Bill reached the trailing rope and gave a pull, saying,

"Come here, Pinto," and with a bound, the horse went to him.

Cayuse Bill's friends were very surprised to see this. I climbed down from my horse and put a loop on Pinto's nose with my rope, then patted his neck and shoulders and walked in a circle. Pinto followed me like a pet dog.

Cayuse Bill said proudly, "That fellow is all horse, and he belongs to me."

When our outfit left the river crossing and started down the Indian trail, I could hear Pinto whinnying for his mates. The rest of the horses that were left behind, tied to trees, were behaving badly for the first time in their lives. The crew all sported fresh rope burns as souvenirs.

The construction camp had been cleaned out of cash, and the poker games could not go on. The men who had not been interested in buying horses were very sore to see the cash leave their camp and hadn't minded letting us know how they felt.

As the outfit moved westward, I was smiling. Now we could keep the chuck box filled again.

The next morning we travelled on an Indian trail. A cut line more-or-less followed this trail through the woods for forty miles. The trail wound from left to right, crossing the cut line every few miles. The new line was chopped out sixty-six feet wide, with stumps standing for miles on end.

A few days later, we found that the stumps along the trail had been pulled. Now the horses could travel on the cut line and make better time than on the narrow trail. But the wagons could not travel here because there were steep water runs and no culverts. They had to continue on the Indian trail. When we ran across a few miles where the stumps had not been pulled, we returned with the herd to the old Indian trail.

Wasps and yellow hornets were spaced at short intervals along this cut line. The insects built nests, which looked like paper sacks, under leaves on the ground, and would pop angrily out of their hives to attack the horses. The animals switched their tails and ran. This was usually timed just right to catch us riders. The herd would barely pass one hive before it tramped over another. We had complained bitterly about the swarms of mosquitoes, but these wasps were the most ferocious pests we had ever encountered.

We had not seen a house of any kind for more than sixty miles. The only sign of any habitation was some thick bark that had been hewed off a tree in six-foot widths and then placed in a cone shape. It was wide enough for a man to crawl inside with a blanket. We guessed it must have been a night camp for one of the stump pullers.

Big George and Whalebone were detained many times. The dry poles that covered the water runs had seen too many summers and many long winters. Occasionally, the boys had to patch a hole. Many unsafe crossings had to be retopped with poplar poles.

The days were no longer so hot, and the evenings were starting to cool. Our progress was very slow. We would make camp in the evening with big hopes of an early start the next day only to be disappointed. Sometimes it took all day to locate the horse herd, and then it was too late to move on.

This stretch of trail was in bear country. Early one morning, Rawhide and Little Bill were rounding up horses a couple of miles back from the cut line when they saw a blackish brown bear. Little Bill told us, "That old bruin galloped away like a horse. It made peculiar grunts as it ran, but we ran just as fast in the opposite direction. Perhaps we made more grunting noises than the bear, as neither of us had a rifle."

The smell of bear seemed to frighten the horse herd. No doubt it was bears that caused the herd to spread so far at night. It was useless trying to night herd in this terrain. Some evenings we heard wolves howling. Often, the riders heard the screech of a wild cat. These sounds, at close quarters, could almost make a prairie boy's hair stand up, so we looked for each other's company and kept our firearms handy.

Small wild hay meadows were frequently found scattered beyond the trail, and the horses were able to gain in flesh and to rest from their miles of travel. But the outfit made only about forty miles in seven days through this area.

I had written a letter to my brother, Seth, and mailed it at High Prairie about ten days earlier. Seth lived on a homestead in northern

British Columbia near Peavine Lake, south of Pouce Coupé, the last
town on the railroad.

I wrote:

> *Good health and fair luck have been with us all the way. The*
> *horse herd is coming through in reasonably good flesh. The boys*
> *of the crew are a great bunch of fellows. We are undertaking to*
> *cross a wild, unsettled territory toward Sturgeon Lake. Some*
> *rivers in that area have no bridges, but the Big Smoky has a*
> *ferry. We are westward bound and hope to see you and land*
> *all our horses safely before the weather gets cold.*

I finished the letter by sending my love to my sister, Eva, and
brother-in-law, Dan Smith. I signed it, "The Mustang Wranglers."

As we got closer to Sturgeon Lake, visitors began to show up at
our camp once more. One day, a man and his wife appeared,
claiming to be Montana people. They spoke of places in Montana
that some of the crew knew very well. The couple tried to persuade
us to locate ourselves right where we were.

"The soil is just as good here as you will find anywhere in the
brush," said the man. "Prospects are very fine here. Potatoes grow
as large as your boots, and the woods are full of wild honey. There
are berry patches for a hundred miles. The blueberries and cran-
berries will soon be in season. Now is the time you fellows should
be looking out for winter.

The homesteader's wife sat on a log and made a fair speech to
us, praising the things the country had to offer. "My husband and I
have been here for only two years, and we have about three acres
cleared of brush and logs. We have a decent log house and a log
barn. If we had a team of horses, we could have done much better."

We were all quiet, listening to what was being said. I wondered
if they weren't more interested in the horses than us. The longer I
listened, the less I felt like staying.

I explained, "We are really looking for country that is a little more
open, where the sun can hit the ground and grow some grass. We are
headed to a country of spring water and unsurveyed wilderness.

We'll have free range there until the country is surveyed. Then we'll lease it from the government. These boys will have the biggest horse ranch in British Columbia by that time. We've seen dozens of places similar to this on our travels, but we didn't stop."

The homesteaders spoke to Big George. "It's a shame for a man of your age to travel so far on a wagon, day after day. What do you intend to do when you get to where you're heading?"

"I guess I haven't thought a great deal about it," Big George responded. "Maybe I'll sleep part of the time. I'll take my shotgun and shoot some rabbits and partridge. I may chop a little wood for Whalebone for my board, or I may take a job with a farmer. After the depression gets past, I may go back to Quebec for a visit. I'm really on my holidays, and it doesn't matter much where I lay myself down."

Before the settler and his wife left our horse camp, they had talked Big George into staying with them.

"Curly, what do you think of this? You fellows are all my best friends, the best a man could have, but I haven't felt real good since we got wet in that river. I have corns on my backside from the wagon ride over this Indian trail. The wagon wheels just jump from one stub of stump onto another. I must be feeling my age lately. These folks have promised to look after me their very best. What do you say, cowboy?"

"Big boy, I would be awfully sorry to lose you from the crew, but you should know your own business. That settler told us there was grass and water three miles west of here, so that's where we'll camp for the night. We'll move along, and you can decide in the next three miles."

By the time we reached the small grass meadow, Big George had made up his mind to stay with the homesteader and his wife.

"If you're determined to stay here," I told him, "I'll have the boys deliver your extra horses back to their log stable. You gather up your belongings from the wagon, and Rawhide and I will separate your horses. If by any chance you change your mind, we'll give you a deadline. We'll stay here until nine o'clock tomorrow morning. If you want to come back, we'll all be happy. If you don't come back by then, we'll know that you intend to stay."

Whalebone set up the tent alone. Big George was busy hunting for his belongings in the wagon while we riders cut out his horses.

It was nearly seven o'clock when Big George drove his wagon into the homesteaders' clearing and stopped beside the log stable. When he unhitched his team we trailed the horses back and turned them loose among the dead windfalls.

When it was time for Big George to bid us goodbye, he said, "I sure hope I'm doing the proper thing. Will you boys promise to write to me when you get to the new ranch?"

"What's the name of the post office here?" Rawhide asked.

"Holy cow," replied Big George. "I have no idea. I sure hope it isn't High Prairie. I don't want to cross that river any more. I'll find out, and you can write it down."

None of us felt like singing around the campfire that night. There was sadness in our hearts because our old friend had left us. We felt as if the big fellow was left all alone in the sticks with perfect strangers who did not appear to be perfect in any way.

Little Bill said, "Fellows, I'm sure glad that Curly gave Big George a deadline. If he gets homesick for us, he can come back. I hope they'll be good to the old fellow. He never had a woman to look after him since he left his mother. I feel quite sure that fellow's wife either wanted him, his horses, or grubstake for the winter."

Rawhide said, "I'll bet they have that old boy out picking berries tomorrow morning at sunrise."

Whalebone chirped, "If we don't leave camp before nine o'clock tomorrow morning, I'll have all you fellows picking berries in the early hours, too. The way you all eat fruit, I can't keep up the supply alone."

At about five o'clock the next morning, before the crew had started to stir much, Big George came into camp on foot. He had hurried for fear of missing us. He was convinced he'd made a mistake. He seemed nervous, lonesome, and hungry as a bear. His first words were, "Curly, they stole my dog. I slept outside on the ground last night, and I've had nothing to eat since dinner yesterday. I think that homesteader intended to rob me. Will you take me back there right after breakfast? I've been an awful fool putting trust in those people. Do you know they expected that I was a million-aire? If I was right sure he stole my dog, I think I would strangle him. Dogs are not used for pack animals around here, but I don't want my dog abused."

We all felt bad about the dog. "Cheer up, big boy," I told him. "The dog chewed a rope in two when the Indians had him back in Athabaska. He'll likely be on your wagon tracks before tomorrow night. He won't be happy without Whalebone's good meals. I bet he'll track us all the way to the mountains if he doesn't get away before."

I spoke to the riders as they washed for breakfast. "One of you cowpokes, saddle Pigeon for Big George when you change horses this morning. He can ride her back for his wagon and bed roll. A couple of us will wrangle his horses out of the brush if they're not stolen, too. In that case, there will be hell popping. We didn't come this far to have some slick guy play around with us. We'll deal fairly with everyone, but the fellow that is deliberately trying to gouge our old friend will be left with something to remember."

Whalebone shouted, "Catch a horse for me too, boys, in case we have to do some tracking. I want to be there."

"We're just sure of the dog being gone," I answered. "Maybe the horses are all there. Anyhow, we can't all leave camp. Someone has to gather the horses and keep an eye on things."

"You can stay here, Curly," shouted Whalebone. "I'd like to ask that man a few questions about our dog."

It was mid-afternoon by the time our outfit started to move west again. We were all glad to have Big George back. We had found his horses and wagon intact, but the old black dog was nowhere to be seen.

Late that night, we camped on an Indian reserve near a set of pole rodeo corrals.

The Cook Rides
the Forty-Four Mare

WHENEVER RAWHIDE SAW A STOCK CORRAL, IT SEEMED to make him bronc-hungry. This morning, he was inspecting the Indians' rodeo corrals when a thought came to him. He soon found me and explained what was on his mind.

"Curly, here's a good place to start another horse. I know we haven't time this morning to tackle any for the saddle, but I have a grey mare I'd like to have harness-broken. I'd like to break her myself. I wonder if Whalebone would let me drive the chuck wagon today, and he could ride in my place. I'll need some more work horses when we get located. This mare could be well broken by the time we get there."

"I'll have a talk with Whalebone," I told him. "I think he'd like a change after the miles he's bumped along on that wagon."

Whalebone was delighted to make the change and started to sing, "I'm an old cowhand from the Rio Grande."

When breakfast was over, Rawhide took possession of the rodeo corrals. With a little help from me, he soon had the horse's hind foot tied up in such a position that he could pull her tail without being kicked. He sacked her out with a bag and rubbed her feet. By the time everything was packed into the chuck wagon, he had the grey mare harnessed and snubbed to a stout wagon horse. Whalebone helped hitch the horses to the chuck wagon.

On one side, the bronco mare was snubbed to my saddle horn. On the other side, she was tied to the ring of the wagon horse. Rawhide was smiling as he gathered his lines and climbed aboard the covered wagon.

"Which direction do we go from here?" he asked.

"For gosh sakes, cowboy," shouted Little Bill, "don't get on the wrong trail and get that chuck wagon lost again. When your horses get tired of running, you better roll that stove off and have dinner cooked for us."

Rawhide looked at his pal and made a face to be remembered. Then he looked at me and shouted, "Turn her loose!"

I slipped the rope off and away went the wagon. I galloped close beside the running team for a few miles.

"What horse is Whalebone supposed to ride today?" I asked.

"It's the forty-four mare's turn," shouted Rawhide, "but you tell Whalebone to take his choice of any horse in my string."

The chuck wagon was bouncing as it disappeared behind the trees. When I rode back to the rodeo corrals, the boys were close by with the herd.

"What horse did Rawhide intend to ride today?" asked Whalebone.

"It's the forty-four mare's turn, but Rawhide said to tell you that you could take your choice of any horse in his string. If that's not good enough, you can pick one from my string. You don't need to bother with that brown mare unless you want to."

Whalebone growled, "The brown mare is good enough for me. I feel like I can ride any dang horse in the band. Roll your spurs, fellows, so we can find the chuck wagon before dinner time."

Big George was following the chuck wagon, but he was not moving very fast. He watched the trail closely for part of the stove or a bed roll that might have bounced off. He remembered the speed of the wagon as it went out of sight and worried that a wheel might fly off and he would find Rawhide sitting along the trail. But then he laughed as he thought, That kid would ride a wagon wheel before he would be stuck very long.

Big George's mind moved on to other things but soon returned to the lad up ahead. That boy won't be sitting anywhere, he thought, but up behind that grey bronco mare. I better hustle along and catch up to him so I can help him get unhitched from the chuck wagon.

I changed my saddle horse for a fresh one and put the forty-four mare in the corral for Whalebone. Then I helped Little Bill get the big band of horses started down the trail.

When I returned to the corral, Whalebone had the brown mare in a three-cornered pen. I led my saddle horse through the gate into the arena and watched through the cracks of the pole fence. Whalebone was trying his best to catch the mare, but she was afraid of him and would not let him get near her.

Whalebone walked over to the fence, where he had placed his saddle, and unbuckled his catch rope. Then he built a fairly large loop, intending to save time. The mare seemed to spook and galloped around in the three-cornered pen. As she passed, Whalebone threw his rope. The mare ducked her head as the loop went over, but when the slack was pulled out of the rope, it tightened around the horse's neck. One front leg was also through the loop. The mare kicked, bucked, and went around that small pen so fast that Whalebone was obliged to climb onto the fence to keep from being run over.

"Can I help?" I shouted.

From the top of the fence, Whalebone replied, "Oh no, she'll be all right in a minute. She's gentle. I just spooked her."

I had ridden this forty-four mare on several occasions and used her once when I was night herding. I had become fairly well acquainted with her and her habits. She was a swell little horse to ride, but she had one terrible fault. She would always try a rider out. Every morning before she would settle down for the day, she would buck about four high pitches and throw herself flat on the ground. If her rider was missing when she got to her feet, she would gallop away and buck a little with an empty saddle. Whalebone had seen this mare perform with the boys several times, and I was hoping he knew what to expect.

I watched closely through the fence as Whalebone placed his saddle on her back. The mare's muscles were tight from excitement.

When Whalebone pulled his latigo to snug up the cinch, she snorted, bucked a little, and stepped on his foot. The cook hopped around for a second or two, while I laughed.

He tightened his cinch solid, opened the gate, and led his mount through to the big arena. I mounted my pony, ready to haze the mare if necessary.

"You should have picked some other horse," I told Whalebone. "We only have one cook."

"Don't worry about me, Curly. I'm an old hand. If this horse will stay on her feet, we'll get along."

"The kind of tricks that mare pulls could make her a cowboy killer," I warned. "She could break a man's legs. I'll be glad when she gentles out. She could be a valuable horse someday, a top horse for any cowboy."

When Whalebone stepped up into the saddle, the mare turned a few half-flips like a sunfish. Whalebone watched her head and every move she made. Suddenly she came down, kerplunk, on her side. She almost fell hard enough to break her ribs. Whalebone spread his legs as far apart as possible and sat there as she scrambled to her feet. The mare did not hesitate for more than a couple of seconds before repeating the performance with a squeal and groan. She let her legs go loose and again landed on her left side. Whalebone came away from her on the run.

The saddle horn had scraped the shin of his left leg, and it was stinging enough to raise his temper. Before he had stopped running, I heard him say, "That's a hell of a horse for a man to have to ride."

I got off my horse and sat down on the ground while Whalebone continued to cuss. I laughed so hard it hurt.

"Whalebone, we can't change horses now. The herd is miles down the trail. You want me to take her?"

"Hell, no, if I can't ride her after Rawhide has ridden her ten times or more, I'll be walking."

Whalebone began to think about how all this looked and started to smile. "I'll be skinned up as bad as you fellows that ride everyday."

I was still laughing and said, "I don't think she'll buck any more.

I'll gallop around the arena with her. She's likely satisfied for today."

Whalebone shouted, "Whoopee, Curly!" and stepped into the saddle. I jumped my horse to crowd the brown mare, and we loped around the big arena, side by side, for a couple of turns. Then Whalebone stepped down from his horse and opened the gate. He mounted her again with no trouble, and we both galloped in the direction that Little Bill had taken the herd. It wasn't long before we overtook him.

That evening, Whalebone tried hard to deal for the forty-four mare.

"She's so unsafe," Rawhide told him. "I'd hate to deal her to anyone. But I think she'll get over it. If I could use her enough so she would get used to things, I'd like her myself. If I just had her at some of those old prairie brandings and could heel a few calves with her, she would learn quite a lot. If I could do that kind of work with her, I wouldn't sell her for four hundred dollars. As she is now, I wouldn't let anybody else own her."

Rawhide began talking about the future. "I'll have lots of time next summer to train all my half-broken horses. I'll be shipping them back to Edmonton for polo ponies when I'm done with them. Do you suppose a kid like me could ever get started in that kind of business? If I could, I'd sure like to have your help, Curly."

I told my young friend that my help was something he could always count on.

Family at Last

MY LETTER REACHED MY BROTHER, SETH GUNTER, AT Tupper Creek. He was glad to hear from me and took the letter over to our sister Eva. My brother-in-law, Dan Smith, read the letter and studied the map to see where we would be now.

"This letter was written ten days ago," said Seth. "Where would that put them? If they made only ten miles a day that would make a hundred miles. They must be as far as Sturgeon Lake. They'll travel toward that ferry on the Big Smoky. I've heard that's a used trail through there and a fair road to Grande Prairie."

Eva looked at the map for a while. "Here is Sturgeon Lake, and there is High Prairie. How will they cross those rivers between?"

Dan thought it was useless to have his wife worrying about the horse outfit, so he answered, "There is a pretty good trail all the way from here to the Big Smoky and a long way past that."

"That letter names five people," Seth pointed out. "That means we should look for another quarter section to go with section eighteen. That's the best section I've seen on my travels while hunting moose. We better take another walk over there. I think that big moose lick comes out of that section. That's a never-ending supply of water. Its source is the Peavine Creek. All they'll need is another good quarter to set up their ranch."

Dan and Seth agreed that they would take a rifle and an axe and look for more land. They found another good quarter section on seventeen, making five quarters in a block. They also found a few small meadows full of windfalls, where fires had burned. The sun could reach the ground, and red top grass was growing there. They also found a set of moose horns that had been rubbed off against a tree when the moose was shedding. They decided to blaze a trail with their axe so they could find their way back later.

Dan and Seth were well-respected neighbours in the small settlement around Peavine Lake. An early-day trapper, known as Dan Anderson, was the first man to take a claim, fronting the lake shore, in this part of British Columbia. He trapped the unsurveyed wilderness for many years and had a large territory issued to him for his trap line. Now that old age was coming on, he intended to take life a little easier. He convinced Seth that he should take over this trap line in order to earn some revenue during these terrible depression years. Since Seth had covered this large territory in the winter of 1930, he knew where to find the best land, the moose licks, and streams.

Dan and Seth stood on a high point in section eighteen and looked southwest at the snow on the mountains.

"If Curly wants free range for his horses, he should be able to find it here," Dan said. "It's ninety miles to those snow-capped mountains, and there's not a soul living between there and where we're standing. It'll be many years before this land is surveyed. It may never be settled in this century. The Cutbank River is only five or six miles west of here and is another good water supply. After a few more fires in there, the red top will grow enough to summer and winter their horses."

"There are a lot of German settlers moving in here lately," said Seth. "I'm afraid that this piece of good land will be taken before the boys get here."

As Dan and Seth walked home, along their blazed track, they talked seriously. Seth said, "Perhaps we should take your Model T and meet the boys. I could ride for a day or two, and you could take Curly to Pouce Coupé to the land office. He could file for the whole crew on section eighteen and this quarter of seventeen. If it doesn't suit them, they can throw it up and file again some other place. It would be a change for us, and maybe our neighbour George Lock would come along. His wife could stay with Eva while we're away."

The next morning, Seth, Dan, and George were on their way to meet the herd. The Ford coupe stopped at Grande Prairie for some gas and oil, and the boys had lunch at the cafe. They made inquiries to see if anyone had seen a large horse herd on the move toward the west. No one had.

The little Ford coupe followed the trail toward the ferry on the Big Smoky. The trail resembled an old Indian trail, and the men in the car didn't make very good time as they were afraid they might break a spring and become stranded.

As the Ford slowly wound its way toward the river, Seth and George were planning a real holiday. George intended to drive a chuck wagon for the first time in his life, but he had no intention of doing the cooking. Seth planned to ride my string of horses and take my place while I went to the land office. Thoughts of the problems they might have catching the horses never entered their heads. It also didn't occur to Seth that half of my string were unbroken horses. They were looking on the bright side of a cowboy's life, with no thought of muskeg, bees' nests, or bruised hides.

Our outfit camped early, in a fair place, about a quarter-mile from the ferry that crossed the Big Smoky River. I met with the ferry operator and made arrangements to load the horses in the morning. We spoke of swimming the herd, but neither of us was in favour of that.

The ferry operator said, "This river is nearly as wide and just as swift as the Peace River. The banks are steep, and the water is cold. If you think you can load them, I'll ferry them over."

Big George built a huge campfire that evening, not far from the wagons. Little Bill's guitar was humming, and songs rang out around the timber. Thoughts of the day were forgotten. It was rest time now, and our bellies were full.

We all missed the black dog. He had not followed the wagon tracks as we had hoped. Big George warned the ferry operator, "If a big black dog ever comes along, please ferry him across, as he may follow yet."

We all shaved and cleaned up, and were entertaining a few Indians, who seemed to enjoy Little Bill's singing. All hands were whooping it up when a Model T Ford coupe rounded a bunch of trees and stopped beside the wagon.

It was a great surprise to see my brother, Seth, and brother-in-law, Dan. We visited while Whalebone got the coffee pot on the stove and made supper for the new arrivals.

Seth told the crew about his plans for me to reach the land office before the piece of good land he had looked at was taken by other settlers. Our plans were well talked over, and the crew was in favour of me doing the business. I asked them to elect a second man to help check out the ranch site. Two heads are better than one. Their next choice was Rawhide.

Dan wanted to return early the next morning. After much back-and-forth conversation, I exclaimed, "You boys can't spare Rawhide and me in the morning. We'll be ferrying horses until at least noon."

Whalebone shouted, "Breakfast is at five. We'll pack up our things after breakfast, and Mr. Lock can drive my wagon. I'll ride the rough string, and Seth can ride the gentle horses."

Seth replied, "I'm no tenderfoot. What Curly rides, I ride."

Whalebone answered, "After we cross the river tomorrow morning, Curly would be riding the Flying Dutchman. I'll tell you, he's no Shetland pony. I don't think he'd like a stranger any better than that leg breaker of Rawhide's."

"When I'm away," I told Seth, "you can ride any of my horses that suit you. There are several good ones in the bunch. There are some half-broken broncs, too. They're used to me, but they're hard to catch and sometimes hard to ride. It's not like the prairie here. When a horse lights out with his head down, you can land up with your knee or your head against a tree. You have a family depending on you, too."

Seth grinned. I was riding broncs when you were in knee pants, he thought to himself.

Whalebone said, "Curly, when you leave here in the morning, don't give us a thought. I know all the horses, and these lads know the trail from here. If you're two or three days away, we'll make out fine. If we reach Grande Prairie before you get back, you'll likely find us celebrating a bit."

Big George grumbled, "River water for four or five more days."

Loading the horses on the ferry was a near science for us, and this time we had three extra men. We repeated our system, time and again, until all the horses were ferried across. Only one horse refused to be loaded, a nice big mare that took to the open river instead of risking her life on the ferry. She heard her mates whinnying across on the opposite bank, and she was determined to get to them on her own power. She swam as straight as the ferry and landed on the far side. But by the time the ferry load reached the landing, we could see that this nice mare had lost her baby colt from the exertion.

I said, "Boys, that's my mare. One of my best. It's a good job we had a ferry on this river. If we had to swim all our herd across here, the herd wouldn't multiply much next spring. Our colt crop would have all been dead and left to feed the bears along the Smoky."

Whalebone had prepared dinner while the horses were being ferried, so we could get rolling. I gave a few important orders and wished everyone luck. Then Rawhide and I sat in the coupe, and Dan started its motor.

After an afternoon ride in the Model T, we began to relax. About nine o'clock that evening, the Ford pulled into Dan's yard. After so long on chuck wagon rations, we enjoyed our supper. It was almost a feast for us. We tried to clear the table of the pies and goodies that Eva had prepared especially for the occasion.

We visited with Eva for a long time before going to bed. She asked many questions about my parents and family. I told her I was expecting to be a daddy, once again, before Christmas, and talked almost continually about my three-year-old, red-headed daughter, Jean, that I was so lonesome for.

I told of an incident along the trail in the woods. "We passed a log cabin where a young mother and her daughter, who was also red-headed, stood watching the big band of horses pass their home. I was riding on the lead when I noticed them. I pulled my saddle

Curly and Jean on Captain. *Courtesy Marlene Davidson*

horse off to the side of the trail and let the herd go by while I talked to them. I held this little two-year-old in my arms, while her mother asked me questions about the prairies. She was raised there, but the depression had driven her and her husband to seek a homestead in the woods, where they could live off the natural resources."

Riding in the Ford was a big change for Rawhide and me after so many miles on a horse. In the morning, though, we were wishing we had a horse to ride, as we dreaded the long walk in riding boots. Dan was ready to take us through the brush to section eighteen.

After tramping for several hours, looking at the windfalls and burned-over country with a big second growth of brush, I said, "There are enough dry logs in these windfalls to build all the buildings for a ranch headquarters. The moose lick coming out of that hill will supply thousands of animals. We may have to grow our hay for the winter until the fires have cleared more land, but right here above this spring would be an ideal place to build. Every morning, we could look southwest and see the snow on the mountains. Ninety miles is close enough. Just right for me."

In the afternoon, Dan drove us to Pouce Coupé. There, we recorded eight hundred acres of British Columbia land to the five wranglers. Dan drove his car back home that evening. He was hoping to get an early start in the morning and deliver us back to the herd. He planned to pick up Seth and George and return home that same night. I had another good visit with my sister and a fair rest from my responsibilities.

The Newspaper
Gets a Story

....

WE REACHED THE HORSE CAMP JUST IN TIME FOR A NOON feed. All were happy to see the car roll in.

Seth was a professional cook, who had cooked for threshing outfits and lumber camps. Now he helped Whalebone turn out new dishes that could be prepared quickly.

When dinner was over, Whalebone said to me, "Well, boy, I'm sure glad to see you back. We had a terrible time catching our horses. They think I'm a stranger, too. We had one runaway with the chuck wagon, but nothing serious. Seth has been riding the Flying Dutchman ever since you left. He hobbles him every time we stop at the wagon. He told me that if you couldn't break your horses any better than that grey, he'd do it for you. So he has rode the grey steady since you left."

"Why did you have a runaway with the wagon?" I asked.

Whalebone spit a little tobacco juice at a pebble and smiled as he said, "Curly, it was that danged old horse of yours, the one with the wings—your Flying Dutchman. The first time Seth mounted him, he took to the air like a toy plane with an elastic band. George had four horses strung out, ready for the road. That grey leaped right into the rigging behind the lead team and ahead of the pole team. Then they all took off. Seth's horse jerked the lead lines away from Mr. Lock, and, boy, did he ever get a ride. Before I had a chance to catch them, they ran straddle of a tree and stopped. Seth's grey tripped on the rigging chains and fell on his nose, but Seth came up with him. The horse wasn't hurt much, just a few of his grey hairs were scraped off from Seth's spurs."

When Dan and his buddies were getting ready for their journey home, Seth said to me, "That grey gelding is getting to be a fair horse now. I'll break him to ride for you when you get into Peavine country. All he needs is a man to handle him." Seth was laughing as he stepped into the coupe and closed the door.

The three men in the car stopped in Grande Prairie, had lunch, and visited the newspaper office, where they gave the editor a big story about five men coming through the woods for weeks, swimming rivers, dodging trains, and pulling muskegs. They said, "That trail herd should be along here in a couple of days. Take some pictures and send us a copy of your paper." The newspaper publisher seemed interested and said he would be on the lookout for the riders.

The men in the Ford were well satisfied that a story would be printed. It would go on record for future generations. They were happy to get home that night, and they told Eva all about their experiences.

Grande Prairie was a wholesale town that distributed goods of various kinds to surrounding communities. Already, its streets were paved. The country was more open, as this district had been settled for many years. Farmers grew grain of different varieties and raised cattle and hogs. To us riders, it looked like most of the livestock were dairy cows, used to supply milk to the growing town. The country had been very prosperous before the depression got its hold on western Canada.

The newspaper people did not want to miss getting a story from us horse wranglers. One morning, they sent a couple of men with a car to find our outfit.

When the newsmen arrived, I was riding on the lead with horses strung out behind me for nearly a quarter of a mile. The two lads were bringing up the herd from the rear. Both wagons were following behind them. The men hailed me and parked their car on the

Saskatchewan Men Trek 1200 Miles to Promised Land

Herding some eighty head of horses, a party of eight arrived in Grande Prairie on Sunday last, after trekking the entire distance from Ponteix, Saskatchewan, a distance of 1200 miles.

Seen by *The Herald* man as they were camped a few miles west of town, the visitors stated that they were bound for a spot eight miles south of Swan Lake.

"Dried out?" asked the reporter.

"Yes," replied one of the party.

"And blown out," added one of the younger members.

The newcomers were D.A. Smith, Blake Powell, Russell and Seth Gunter, Ed Torrance, George Patineau, Wm. Colby, and George Lock.

The strangers were being piloted by Seth Gunter, who was in the country last year and picked out the area to which the party was going.

The Saskatchewan men came well prepared for their long journey. There was a chuck wagon, with plenty of chuck in it. In fact, they had everything necessary for the long trip.

"How do you like this part of the world?" was one of the questions put by *The Herald* man. "How do we like it?" replied one of the party, "Say, you can tell the world through that paper of yours that we are here to stay." "Lots of feed here," replied another.

Were they down-hearted? Certainly not. They had arrived in the promised land, thanks to their Moses, Seth Gunter, who, as stated above, spied out the land.

Discussing their long march, the newcomers stated that they had a good trip. Only on three occasions were they delayed, and that was when some of the horses strayed away.

As *The Herald* man walked away, one of the men shouted, "Send us a copy of the paper. We will all be subscribers as soon as we get settled."

The newcomers are of the type most needed in this country. They are real products of the land and have in a marked degree adaptability so necessary to the success of pioneers in these parts.

Grande Prairie *Herald*
18 September 1931

side of the trail. Each rider, in turn, was questioned. When the wagon men came along, they were questioned, too. Whalebone took a fresh chew of tobacco and strung them a long line.

When we reached Grande Prairie, we skirted the town on account of traffic and trains. It was late in the evening, but we kept on. No one wanted another night like the one in Swift Current.

About four or five miles west of Grande Prairie, we found a fair place to camp with enough grass to allow us to stay over one day. We were able to get into town and fill the chuck box once more, as well as pick up our mail, which we were all anxious to do. Big George managed to forget about his dog for a while, as he had no intention of drinking river water when there was something stronger available.

Many folks had already read accounts of the herd. The wrangler story took up most of the front page of the paper. It appeared that the three men in the Ford had come ahead to the new country. These fellows were classified as "Moses leading the Israelites into the promised land." History was repeating itself.

By noon, the camp had company. Little Bill entertained them with music and song for some time, then showed how he could lead our mascot, the colt, into a high wagon. The young cowboy placed an arm around the little horse's neck, walked her toward the wagon, and placed the colt's front feet into the box, one at a time. Then he gently placed his hand behind the colt's rump to give her a little boost. The colt jumped into the wagon box, the end gate was put in place, and the little filly was ready to ride all day with her mother following not far behind.

I began to study my map closely. Roads were much better and settlements were closer together from Grande Prairie to the British Columbia border. The crops were tall and thick, and we saw threshing machines working in several communities. The farmers we met all had about the same story to tell of farming conditions. They all agreed it would cost more to take the harvest off than what they would receive from its sale.

A couple of days before entering the district of Hythe, in western Alberta, we camped in a place that had an abundance of grass but no water. I seldom allowed this to happen, as water seemed to be my main concern. Our camp was pitched on high ground, not far from an experimental farm at Beaver Lodge. Over the top of a forest of trees we could see a lake, about three miles away. With much effort, we took all the horses there for a drink, but when we reached the lake, we found that the shore was terribly boggy. Not even deer could drink. The herd seemed to be in a bad way for water this morning so we galloped and shouted to turn the horses back, but some stragglers were determined to try the lake. We all had visions of what would happen if the horses were to bog here.

While returning to our camp with the thirsty horses, we met a stranger who told us, "If you go north of town, you'll see a large hill known as Saskatoon Mountain. I've been told that water seeps out on the north side and runs down the hill."

We thanked the stranger and trailed back to camp. I called to Whalebone and Big George, "We're taking the herd to Saskatoon Mountain for water. That lake was so boggy we couldn't even get a drink ourselves. I don't suppose you have a gallon of coffee for us before we go?"

When we reached Saskatoon Mountain, water seeped so slowly that the horses had tramped it into a mud hole before they were able to quench their thirst. I was worried. For a day or two now, I had not been satisfied with the water supply for the horses. So that evening I set out on my favourite horse to look for water. I left the main road and had ridden about two miles south when I came to a farmyard. I made myself acquainted and asked about water. The farmer replied, "You're welcome to all the water you want. Just help yourself. There's a tub there that holds about twenty gallons." He pointed toward a pipe that stuck out of the ground about sixteen inches. There was a small amount of water running into the tub and overflowing in a tiny stream toward a swamp.

I thanked him and replied, "I don't only want to have a drink for me and my horse, I'd like to find water for a big herd of one hundred head."

The farmer smiled and said, "Great Scott, you'll be all night watering at that tub."

"I guess I would," I replied. "They are nearly all broncs, and I don't think any of them would go near the tub. Some of the horses would choke for water first. Do you suppose I could bank up the stream with a shovel? Maybe they would drink from the ground."

The farmer answered, "You might try that if you like. There's a shovel right here beside the stable."

I took the shovel and started to make a small dike across the water course. While I worked, I answered questions from the farmer's five young children. Toward the swamp, I could see four or five big sows waddling through the mud. I hoped that these pigs would not root up what I was so busy building. After working about an hour, I decided that the reservoir was filling up. The best thing to do was to get the herd here before dark, or they would never find this new dam.

The gang was lying on the ground between the wagon and Big George's large bonfire, smoking and telling yarns. They jumped to their feet when they saw me and asked if I had found anything.

I explained, "I borrowed a shovel from a farmer, made a dike across a water run, and let it fill up. It's right in the farmer's yard. There are flower beds, gardens, kids, dogs, hogs, chickens, and everything else that belongs in a farmyard. We'll have to be very careful. I hope the kids will be in bed when we get there."

The two riders and I took the horses to the water. The reservoir was nearly full, and part of the bunch got a good drink. Those that were very nervous kept stepping in and out until my mud dam was completely tramped out. This left a small trickle running through the mud toward the swamp.

Apparently, there were a number of artesian wells in the area surrounding Hythe. Scarcity of water never entered the farmer's thoughts. All he needed to do was hold a pail under a spout for a few seconds. He had a reservoir or tub that held more than twenty gallons, and the surplus water drained away in shallow pools. These pools were deep enough to water a few pigs and chickens, and in this case, quite a few horses.

The End
of the Trail

A FEW MILES WEST OF HYTHE, OUR OUTFIT CAMPED IN A large clearing that resembled the open prairie, on the Horse Lake Indian reserve. In the spring, this open spot was a lake, but as the shallow water seeped away, it became a wonderful hay meadow. We counted several haystacks around the meadow and a small lake in the centre.

While looking at these haystacks, I got an idea that the Peavine Ranch was not so far from here. I thought perhaps I could make some kind of a deal for a few haystacks. The herd could be wintered here when the snow got too deep for them to forage.

I talked a deal with a young Indian who was visiting the camp and listening to Little Bill's songs. The man, who lived close by, said, "Sure, Mister, I'll trade ten stacks for some horses."

Before the deal was made, I thought that the Indian's agent should be consulted, but by the time the agent was located, the lad was missing. The agent told me, "Nearly all that hay is sold. Once in a while, people can be rascals, so if you have any dealings here, it is as well to have it okayed by me."

Farther along the road, some big straw- and oat-sheave stacks appeared. I looked over the map to see how far this was from the Peavine Lake country.

"Listen, boys," I said, "we're only about thirty miles from our new ranch, providing we have a road straight across. If we follow this road and the railroad, it might be fifty. That's not far for our breed of horses. I hope we don't have to feed before Christmas. I certainly don't know anything about the range in this part of the world."

Big George smiled when he heard me say it might be only fifty more miles. He looked at the map for a few minutes, then whispered, "The next little village we pass is Demmitt. I wonder how big a place that is. Surely they don't have to drink river water there."

Rawhide piped in, "That place isn't far from Swan Lake. It's just across the border. I hope there are hay meadows there, too. Tupper Creek is situated on the end of Swan Lake, not far from Seth's homestead. We were there a couple of times in the Ford."

The small village of Demmitt was built on top of a hill, overlooking the railroad tracks. In the valley, which seemed quite clear of trees, we could see a monstrous log pile close to a small saw mill. Near the mill stood a huge pile of sawdust.

Whalebone announced, "We'll be able to get lumber right here, boys. If we build with logs, we'll still need some lumber for a roof and partitions. Tomorrow, we should see the end of our trail. I hope we don't have any more muskeg troubles. I'll be glad when we can turn this bunch of broom tails loose and let them raise their colts like the moose raise their young."

About five o'clock on a Friday afternoon, we turned the horse herd south from the old Peace River Drag and debated whether to camp early, or travel another ten miles and finish our journey. Rawhide and I had been to Peavine Lake before, but both times had been after dark. Neither of us knew our directions, as the coupe had made many turns on several narrow trails. Now we had no idea which trail to take. We decided the surest thing to do was camp and move on in the daylight.

The horses were turned loose to graze as we set up camp. We intended to celebrate our last evening meal from the end of the roundup wagon.

Horses spread around in a big grazing circle, and Big George built another campfire. He brought in such large chunks of wood that he could scarcely drag them to the flames. He told the boys, "The Indians make a small fire and get right over it, but I like to make a big one and stand back where I can watch the flames."

When supper was over, I saddled my horse and rode circles around the grazing herd. When I returned, I reported that everything was in order for the night.

I spoke quietly to the men around the campfire, "Just one more day to go lads. Tomorrow night, we'll sleep in Seth's log house. We'll put our feet under a table and eat like gentlemen. If we can find the proper trail in the morning, we should be entirely finished with this drive. Nobody looks any worse than when we started."

The next morning, Whalebone had the crew up early and fed us breakfast before the squirrels awoke.

"I'll inquire from a settler about the road, and Big George and I can go on with the wagons. There are narrow cut lines running in every direction, but surely somebody knows the country. We'll get moving right away."

Whalebone was loading the groceries and bed rolls when Little Bill galloped into camp with reports of missing horses.

Big George groaned, "More muskeg, I'll bet."

Rawhide and I had fresh horses saddled, and it didn't take long to mount them and get riding. We found a small bunch of horses back on the north side of the highway, not far from Swan Lake. We made a general roundup and took a new count. After several counts, we were still short two head. We imagined the horses in a muskeg, near dead from exhaustion. Where the brush was not too thick, we galloped in to search, but no muskeg or strayed horses were found.

Rawhide was riding in sight of the highway and noticed a car coming from the east, so he galloped to the road and hailed the driver. "Have you seen any stray horses on your travels?" he asked.

The stranger told him, "The only horses I've seen today were two head, away back east of Demmitt. They were on the railroad tracks, going east at one heck of a clip, ahead of the train."

Rawhide tilted his hat to the back of his head as he thought about this. "That sounds like ours. We're only short two horses." He thanked the stranger and, at once, rode south to find me.

I looked disgusted as Rawhide related the story.

"The stranger said that the engineer was pulling the whistle to see those horses run. If they stay on the tracks, we may have to ride to Grande Prairie before we find them," he said.

Before I started toward camp, I turned my horse and spoke to my pal. "Better catch yourself a fresh horse, Rawhide. Find a good long-winded one that likes to travel. Catch a good tough one for me. I'm going to the wagon to tell Whalebone not to move away from this camp. I'll have Little Bill hold the herd farther south, away from any more trains. I'll be with you before you catch those fresh horses."

I rode to the chuck wagon and said quickly, "Whalebone, don't move from here until we come back. If Little Bill needs a hand, you take a horse and help him. He can hold the horses south of camp this morning. We have two runaway horses on the railway track, away back at Demmitt. They were heading east, ahead of the train."

Before the cook could find his tongue, I was gone.

Rawhide and I made good time going toward Demmitt. He rode a long-legged, long-winded bay gelding, and I rode Pigeon. We followed the edge of the highway at a steady lope. We were both thinking how nice it would be once we got the herd into the unsurveyed territory, away from the trains.

Our thoughts returned to the horses that were ahead of the train. I sighed. "It seems to me that that track was fenced with slabs where we crossed the herd yesterday. I hope those fan tails won't break a leg and have to be killed. I left my rifle at the wagon."

At that moment, Rawhide shouted, "I can see two horses over there on the tracks. They're coming this way. The way they're travelling, I'll bet there's another train not far behind them. Let's cut across here and head them off."

When the sweating horses were halted, we looked at their brands. Both were wearing my G Half Diamond on their left hip. Rawhide smiled when he saw them and sort of whispered, "I'd know that pair of mares anywhere, even if it was dark and I couldn't see their brands. Those two are half wild. That train must have run the devil out of them. Just look at them sweat."

"They're gaunt," I answered, "and they look like they just swam the Big Smoky. Let's get them back to the highway before another train runs us all down. Pigeon is nearly scared to death of trains."

Rawhide and I had a big appetite and a very late dinner. The herd was well filled and fresh from their rest. We were determined to reach Peavine Creek today, and saddled fresh ponies for the last lap of our journey.

Everybody seemed very pleased with the long drive. We had pulled numerous muskegs, night herded in bear country, camped against cities, crossed all the big rivers of the North country, and the horses had even escaped being injured when the tree fell across the corral at Athabaska.

Today's count proved that we had not lost one animal. Some had been sold along the way, but they were all accounted for. We were in far better condition than we had ever been. Big George felt weary but had gained at least another ten pounds. The chuck box still contained a good supply of provisions, and as Rawhide said, "No man of our crew has missed a meal since we left Val Marie—but we had to postpone a few."

That evening, about late suppertime, the horses crossed Peavine Creek, and we let them go for the night. The chuck wagon stopped beside Seth's log house, which we would all call home until other arrangements were made.

We had reached "the promised land."

A Warm Welcome

MY BROTHER, SETH, HAD LEFT HIS FAMILY IN PONTEIX, Saskatchewan, while he travelled the Peace River country in search of new stamping grounds. As mentioned earlier, Seth had settled beside an old trapper who was ready to retire and had taken over the old fellow's large trap line. My sister, Eva, and brother-in-law, Dan Smith, also lived nearby. Seth and Dan built two warm log houses of good size and had some of the best spring water in the area. It ran out of the ground and flowed into Peavine Lake. There was another small stream of cold water running across both homesteads, where anyone could lie on their belly and get a cold drink on a summer day. Seth had a number of straight logs cut and was prepared to add on to his house. His family, including his wife and five children, were coming to join him before Christmas.

Seth made an offer to the boys. "If you help me hoist up my logs to be notched and fitted into place, I'll do the carpenter work for you when you're ready to build." The boys were pleased to have help from someone who could hew a corner straight and accepted his offer thankfully.

Eva and Dan lived about two hundred feet from Seth's house. Eva had a real home-cooked meal prepared for our first supper there. After we ate, I helped with the dishes, and we visited a good deal while Eva's dog, a big German Shepherd, kept an eye on us. The dog's name was Tex, and if her name was mentioned, she came at once. She was a good friend to some people and a terrible foe to others. The dog acted as Eva's bodyguard when she was alone in the woods in this new frontier.

Seth had a word with us after supper. "I have a fair-sized stable, a pole corral, and a stack of hay," he said. "You can help yourselves. I also have a hundred acres of hay growing around the lake, though I haven't taken most of the logs and brush out of it yet. It should've been hayed a couple of months ago, but you fellows can use it anyhow. On Monday morning, you'd better get your mower working. By changing horses often enough, a lot of feed can be salvaged before the snow. We'll make a bucking pole and stack the hay on a high point beside the meadow.

"George Lock has only one horse and about a ton of peavine that he cut by hand. It's coiled up in piles. If you boys will get me a team in the morning, I'll go over there and haul that in for him before your horses find it. There is nothing else around this country that your horses can harm."

That night, a surprise party was staged at Dan and Eva's house with all the neighbours in attendance—a "get-acquainted party" Eva called it. Among the crowd were bachelors, married couples, young and old. All had left good homes to move here on account of the depression.

Little Bill stole the show, as usual, with his entertaining. Others sang, recited, and did magic tricks. The crew all enjoyed a warm welcome.

Two night horses were kept in the stable with a manger of hay, while the big bunch grazed the peavine among the trees. Rawhide and I planned to take a count in the morning to make sure none of the horses had backtracked or found a muskeg. We hoped that the herd would soon locate themselves.

Big George was happy as he rolled into bed on Saturday night. He had made new friends, and he was thinking about taking a short rest.

"No wagon to grease tomorrow morning. I doubt very much if I'll ride a wagon any more this year. I'll sleep, hunt, and fish. I might even pitch a little hay, but no more wagon seat for me. A good walk

Eva and Dan Smith, 1932.
Courtesy Marlene Davidson

is what I need to limber me up and take some of the cramps out of my muscles. Tomorrow, I'll shoot some grouse for Whalebone. It won't be hard to get meat in this part of the world," he told us.

Whalebone was also talking more than usual. "A month ago, I thought we'd have to eat pony, but I've seen several moose lately. I haven't heard a wolf howl since we left the Smoky. This must be Saturday night; it's hard to keep track of the days. It seems like a year ago since we left Val Marie."

I listened closely to the boys' conversation. I, too, was ready for bed. I smiled and spoke to the sleepy bunch of men. "Fellows, we have had a two-month-and-ten-day vacation. Now, we'll go to work. The weather isn't hot any more, and there are no mosquitoes to bother us. We can get the mower going on Monday. The best axe man can do some house planning and help Seth. He'll show you fellows how to fall a tree and not be under it."

Seth roused himself on his elbow and said, "I'm adding another forty feet to this place and I already have every log cut. I'll need some help to skid them in here and lift them up. I know where there are enough good straight logs to build each of you a house. It won't take us long to put up the outside if some of you guys will work with Dan and me."

We Lose
Big George

O N SUNDAY MORNING, WHALEBONE COULD NOT STAY IN bed. He was thinking of his new house with the bearskin rug and of his school marm and her cooking. He strode out to the chuck wagon, got his sourdough crock, and took it into the house. Before long, the hotcakes were stacked up, and eggs and bacon were frying in the pan. He whistled as he worked.

"You fellows will find a wash basin outside by the door," he told us. "Get out there and wash some sleep from your eyes. Roll your spurs. We're in British Columbia now, and we'll have to make use of the daylight for a while. You can sleep next winter after our work is done."

We were all in good humour as we gathered around Seth's table for breakfast and joked with each other. Our appetites seemed better than ever, if that was possible.

Whalebone remarked, "Seth's meat house is full of meat, and he told me to help myself. Before that begins to get low, I'm going to shoot another moose or two and fill it up again. If each one of us gets our quota, we should have meat for a year."

When breakfast was finished, we went into the yard. It was warm in the sun, and there was no breeze.

Little Bill tacked a bull's-eye target onto a square piece of board and nailed it to a tree. Then he took a pencil and made several circles around the bull's-eye, and, as he was always full of fun, he challenged Rawhide to a small bet. They were using Whalebone's six-shooter.

Big George paced off about sixty feet, making a mark on the ground. Rawhide borrowed the Luger and a handful of shells, and they started to shoot. They each took three shots, but neither of them hit the bull's-eye. Some bullets even missed the circles. The bet was even. Little Bill brought out his twenty-two calibre rifle, and everybody took one shot, blotting out the bull's-eye.

Rawhide and I saddled our ponies outside of the stable. We wanted to look at the horses and take a count.

"If you boys will bring in a gentle team for me," Seth shouted, "I'll haul that hay for my neighbour this morning."

Rawhide answered, "Fine, we'll have a team to you by eight-thirty. Have the boys lift off the wagon box and put on the rack. We won't be long." Before eight-thirty, we were back with a gentle team.

Big George gazed at some horses that were on a burned-over side hill about half a mile away. He thought, The sun is warm and it's too nice to sit around. I'll take my promised walk and see what sort of grazing those horses have. Maybe I'll take the little rifle with me and bring back some partridge. It's Sunday, so we won't work today, and I need a little exercise.

We were one happy bunch as we sat eating breakfast. We were all looking forward to working together as a family. The silver lining of the cloud was shining through; the dark spots were in the past. The journey that so many thought impossible was finished.

Little Bill said, "We'll build a herd between here and those mountains. Just give us another ten years and British Columbia will be on the map for having the finest horses in the nation.

"The first time we go to Pouce Coupé, Rawhide and I will register our British Columbia horse brand. When we brand our next year's crop of colts, they'll wear a TC on their left hip. That will be a brand to be proud of."

Big plans were being made. Whalebone sounded like a man with much ambition.

"When I build my house, I'm going to hew the logs all square. I'll put big windows in the south for plenty of light and am going to build a chimney with stone and mortar. Maybe I'll build a fireplace, too. I intend to build an ice house before spring and I'll make a smoke house like Seth has. Before long, I'll have a few big wild steers roaming the countryside. Someday, I'll ride away back to those mountains and see what I can find. I'll bet there are enough meadows, here and there, to keep you fellows busy cutting hay all summer long."

We were all watching Whalebone and listening with much interest when suddenly Little Bill spoke up. "You'd better wait until your school marm comes before you make that trip. You could make up a pack train and go in there for your honeymoon."

Whalebone rolled a cigarette, smiled, and said, "I think I'll meet her in Edmonton. We'll see the bright lights for a week or two, and then we'll settle down. We'll try to build ourselves a ranch here in these unsurveyed wilds."

Seth hitched his team to the wagon with the rack. As he drove away from his stable, he noticed Big George walking down the trail, carrying a small rifle. He soon overtook the big fellow and asked, "Where are you going?"

Big George looked at him with a large grin, "I haven't much of an idea of my direction, if that's what you mean. I'm just going over there to that side hill where those horses are grazing. I want to see what they have to eat."

Seth said, "That's where I'm going for a load of hay. Hop up here and ride along. By the time you've finished looking around, I'll have my hay loaded. You can ride to the Lock place with me. We'll have a game of five hundred, and then you can come back home with me."

Big George declined the offer. "Thanks, Seth, but I'd rather get a little exercise, and maybe I'll scare up some partridge. I'll take a walk around those horses and be back home in an hour."

Big George walked beside Seth's wagon and talked until the trail crossed a small spring-fed creek with a long culvert. The creek flowed gently across Seth's homestead. Big George, who was used to drinking river water, flopped down on his belly and drank from the cool, clear spring.

"Look west up this creek," Seth told him. "You can see George Lock's log house and stable. That's where I'm taking the hay. It's only about half a mile from here."

Big George looked west where Seth was pointing. "I can see it plainly from this culvert. Maybe I'll come around there and have a chat with George and his wife on my way home."

Meanwhile, Rawhide and I had counted the horses and looked over the range for feed.

"There's a big spring feeding into the lake behind that clump of spruce trees," said Rawhide. "Part of that lake shore is boggy. The creek that starts up there on section eighteen comes into the lake over on that far side. It's a good place for the stock to get water all the way to its source. No bog holes, either."

We separated and each made our own circle, then met again where the creek flowed into the lake. There we dismounted and allowed our ponies to drink their fill while we laid on our bellies and took a good drink ourselves.

"I can't tell north from south in this dang brush country," I said. "I don't want to get very far from a cut line, either. Seth told me that it's easy to go anywhere and get back. He showed me the landmarks on every side of home. That's Chin Whiskers up there behind the lake. He told me that if we ever have doubts about where we are, to look for Chin Whiskers and go toward it. We'd find the lake and a cut line to return home. Don't ever forget about that landmark."

Chin Whiskers was a hill of mountainous proportions, covering a section of land. A large clump of spruce trees grew on the very top of this hill, reaching above the skyline. As this was the highest point in the entire countryside, it could be seen from wherever a person might be.

Rawhide was riding a small wiry and snorty little horse by the name of Donald. Donald had been ridden for the first time in the corrals on the Saskatchewan River. He could run like a rabbit, at full speed from the first jump, and he could dodge like a sheep dog when cutting horses from the herd. He had the good looks and confirmation to be a valuable horse for jobs such as calf roping, picket racing, barrel racing, or even polo. His face, between his eyes, was flat with no fullness, which showed intelligence. He was quick to learn, but also quick to pick up bad habits. When he bucked, a rider who managed to stay on knew he had fire underneath, but Donald would never kick a fallen rider. Rawhide was always careful when handling him and knew that he was well mounted. If he was careless in his actions, he was soon bucked off.

When we left the creek, we separated once more to comb the brush country for more horses to complete our count. We were soon out of each other's sight. In about ten minutes, I heard crashing in the brush that sounded like a running moose or a bear in a hurry. I looked in the direction of the noise and saw Rawhide's bay horse bounding through the brush with an empty saddle. Wondering what had happened to my partner, I soon caught the dragging reins of the horse and stopped him short. In a minute, Rawhide came walking out of the black alder brush carrying a dry stick.

The cowboy smiled sheepishly when he saw me with his horse. "I was riding through that thick alder brush with my eyes shut, and this dry stick ran up my pant leg and broke off," he said. "I leaned over to take the stick out, not even thinking what horse I was riding, and flew the rest of the way to the ground. He never misses a chance to unload me. How many times does that make that he's dumped me?"

I always had to laugh at this kind of excitement. "I can't rightly remember the number of times," I said, "but I remember the first time. Do you remember the day Whalebone was driving some broncs on the chuck wagon, going across a gumbo flat like old Satan was chasing him? A stove lid bounced off the wagon, and when you reached for that stove lid Donald slid you over the gumbo. If I had gotten to the stove lid first, I'd have climbed down and picked it up. I guess you figured that if you got off, he wouldn't let you back on with that black thing. Now, old kid, if you're not hurt, here's your horse."

Rawhide had a scratch or two but was unhurt. He mounted Donald and continued to talk. "This horse has piled me more times than all the rest of my horses put together. I'll gentle him someday, and he'll be a valuable polo pony. He can turn on those hind feet like a rabbit."

I laughed some more at Rawhide, looking at a deep scratch on the side of his nose. "With a little more of that kind of practice," I said, "he'll be valuable for a bareback rodeo horse. I guess you wouldn't have to gentle him much for that."

Before leaving camp, we had seen Whalebone fill the oven with a large moose roast. Once we found the horses, we began to have visions of a roast dinner. Rawhide claimed, "It's the smell of pine and the change in climate that bothers me. I'm forever hungry, and I can eat enough for two men."

"That goes for all of us prairie boys," I said. "Big George can eat like a cow pony. If this keeps up, we'll all be fat old men shortly. Right now, I'm as hungry as a coyote. Let's ride."

When we reached Seth's corrals, we turned our horses in, fed them some hay, and raced to the house for a feed. Whalebone and Little Bill were all alone and dinner was waiting.

"Where's Big George today?" I asked. "Did he go with Seth for the hay?"

Whalebone answered, "It was such a bright morning, and he needed some exercise, so he took the little twenty-two rifle and went for a walk. I think he must be helping Seth with the hay, as neither one has come back."

That afternoon, I spent a few enjoyable hours with Dan and Eva. At about four o'clock, I said, "I must go back and write some letters. My wife will be glad to know that we landed here safely and that everybody is in good health."

When I finished my letter, I noticed that Whalebone and I were alone. I winked at him and said, "You're next." I wrote a short letter for Whalebone, telling of his great plans for the future.

"It's too bad the big fellow isn't here. I'd write a letter to his sister for him, and this mail could all go out in the morning. Dan is going to town with the Ford and could put our letters on the train going east."

Later, I helped prepare supper. As Big George and Seth had not come in yet, I asked, "What time did Seth say he'd be back?"

"When we see him, he'll be here," replied Whalebone. "They're likely having a card game at the neighbour's. They'll be in after a while. Seth knows all the trails through here because he made them all last summer. Those men must have worked hard—Dan and Seth cleared twenty acres or more with their axes. They have brush piles all over."

That evening, Little Bill put on his one-man concert. He was hoping some neighbours would call again, but no one came. At about nine o'clock, we heard the rattle of the wagon.

Rawhide and I went out to help Seth take care of the team. When the wagon stopped, I asked, "Where's Big George? Didn't he go with you?"

Seth replied, "Didn't that old fellow come home? He must be lost. He told me he was coming right back. I haven't seen him since nine o'clock this morning, and that was at the crossing on the small creek. He left me there and didn't show up at the Lock's place. I was sure he'd gone home. Where do you suppose he would go?"

"Do you have any neighbours living in the direction he went?" asked Rawhide.

"Sure," Seth replied. "There are neighbours scattered here and there, all the way to town. But Big George would never find any trails to them from this direction."

Little Bill's music stopped with a crash when he and Whalebone heard the big fellow might be lost. Little Bill ran out of the house and looked at the country of trees. "It's black dark. What are we going to do?" he shouted.

"I'll go out there in the brush and wrangle some saddle stock," exclaimed Rawhide. "It's likely we'll all be lost in this black dark, as Little Bill calls it."

"The first thing we had better do is ask some of our nearby neighbours if they've seen him," said Seth. "He might be visiting with some of them. I'll take one of those ponies from the corral and check. I know where they live and the trails to get there. I won't be long."

Rawhide saddled Donald, and he and Seth rode out into the night on different missions.

When Seth returned, he reported that no one had seen Big George since the party last night. It hadn't taken Seth long to check with the neighbours. He had ridden at a fast lope and didn't stop for more than a minute at any place. We all began to worry about Rawhide being lost, too, but soon we heard him coming with a few horses, which Seth helped corral.

Plans were quickly made to search for Big George. "I'd rather swim the Smoky than ride this strange brush country after dark," I said. "We may all be lost tonight. Each rider should take a handful of matches. If we do get lost, we'll build a big fire and stay there until morning. In the daylight, we should be able to see Chin Whiskers."

Seth said, "Big George doesn't know anything about Chin Whiskers."

"Neither do I," said Little Bill. "What's that?"

After Seth told everyone about the landmark, we set off to look for our friend.

The Manhunt

EVA SET A LIT LAMP IN EACH WINDOW OF HER HOUSE. "It was really nice all day," she said, "but it's cold tonight. I don't believe Big George had a coat when he left here this morning."

"No, he didn't," Seth responded. "He was in shirt sleeves, and they were rolled up past his elbows when I talked to him at the creek. I wonder if he has matches."

I spoke up, "He's a heavy smoker and always carries his pipe. Surely he'll have matches. If he builds a fire, it's sure to be a big one—big enough to set the woods on fire. Big George has been our fire man every night for weeks. If he has matches, he won't freeze, but I'll bet he's hungry. I've had three meals today, and I'm hungry again."

"He's a good shot with his rifle," said Little Bill. "He could shoot a grouse and roast it if he was hungry. If he makes a big fire, we should be able to see it for miles on a dark night like this. We'll find him." But I could see the worry in the young cowboy's eyes.

Seth showed the boys the direction that Big George had taken. "If he went over that burned-over side hill," he said, "the country is all heavy brush. In some places, the black alder grows in clumps like willows. You can't even walk through there."

Dan said, "Listen to me, boys. I have an idea. Seth and I have several good-sized brush piles over there in our clearing. When you fellows ride north, we'll light a brush pile. You'll have the light at your back. We'll keep piling on the brush, and a streak of light will shine high into the sky. When you get out there by the creek, you'd better spread out. Four riders spread a quarter of a mile apart will cover a whole mile. Keep shouting so the next man can hear you, and keep this light at your backs. Look for Big George's campfire. Surely he'll have one by now. He won't walk in a straight line, either. No one knows which way he'll circle. Don't go more than three or four miles or you won't be able to see our light to get back. If he went that way, you'll find him tonight."

When Big George had left the house on this beautiful Sunday morning, little did he know what was in store for him. He had intended to take a stroll and get the kinks out of his legs. He thought the exercise might sharpen his appetite, as he had seen Whalebone put a large roast into the oven. He had shaved, changed his clothes, and left his coat behind, since he did not plan on being away very long.

After the big fellow left Seth at the creek, he sat down for a smoke. He felt in his pocket for his pipe and tobacco but could not find them. He realized that when he had changed his clothes he had forgotten to take his smoking material from his other pockets. He groaned. I'll take a walk around the horses, he thought, then I'll go back by Lock's place. I'll make a cigarette there, and then I'll go home for dinner.

Big George walked up the side of the burned-over hill. From there he could see for half a mile. He looked at the horses that were grazing and thought, Curly sure brought the herd through in good shape. I hope all the range is as good as it is here.

He walked over to an old, burned windfall and sat down. He began to think about his chances in a country like this compared with his farm back on the prairie. If the drought continues for another year or two back there, he thought, and the depression is still riding us with both spurs, we have nothing to lose here. There is lots of wood, water, and meat. I'll get in a few sacks of flour, salt, coffee, beans, and a supply of tobacco. What more would an old bachelor like myself look for? I'll live like a king and be my own boss. I'm among the best friends any man has ever had. I'll work hard until we all get a house built, then I'll play poker with the boys in town and drink a few mugs of beer.

Big George got up from the log and walked slowly, down the hill, at an angle. He wondered if he would have done better to go back to his sister's at Duck Lake. She's a nun in a hospital and wouldn't have much time for me, he thought. She never did want me to go on a party. This will be a gentleman's life out here once we get settled. Tomorrow, I'll sharpen my axe and start to cut some logs.

Big George walked to the floor of the valley and took another drink from the brook. Then he began to look for Lock's place. On the opposite side of the creek from Lock's, Big George could see a log house. I'll get a smoke up there and go home, he decided.

Still thinking hard, he walked through the valley. When he arrived at the log house, he found that no one lived there. There was a padlock on the door. The big boy said aloud, "That's strange. Seth pointed this place out from the creek. I must be turned around somehow."

Suddenly he had a helpless feeling. "It was right here that Seth was taking the hay." He took a look at the sun and wondered what business it had shining from that direction at this time of the morning. He tried to get his bearings, but this put him in a terrible muddle. He didn't know that Seth was only fifty rods away, on the opposite side of the creek. If he had looked across the valley, over the tree tops, he could have seen George Lock's home in the small clearing. If he had shouted then, he might have been heard. But instead, he picked a direction that looked right to him, walked around the house, and entered the alder brush.

The big fellow walked as fast as possible through the brush. He was thinking, I'm not lost yet. I'm only half a mile from home, and I'll make it in time for dinner. Sometime that afternoon, he heard a dog bark and hustled in that direction, feeling a little happier. Although he did not hear the dog bark again, he kept hunting for it.

The afternoon was warm, and Big George became very thirsty but was unable to find the creek. He could hardly remember when he had been so tired and hungry. His mind kept coming back to the large roast that had filled the oven that morning. He kept going, hoping he would soon see the house and clearing.

Before sundown, he was sure that he heard a rooster crowing. When he hurried toward the sound, he found a barbed wire fence in the brush and followed it for nearly half a mile until he saw a faint trail. He followed the trail, looking hard for a house or clearing, until the trail ran out and he was unable to find the fence again. He decided that the trail must have been made by a hunter dragging out a moose. He sat down on a windfall to rest and felt for his pipe, then remembered that he had left it behind. "I can't sit here," he said to himself. "It will be dark in half an hour, and I'm starving."

When the sun went down, it looked far different from a western sunset. I'm lost for sure, thought Big George. If my dog was here, he'd take me home. If I build a fire, Curly will find me before morning. He hunted in his pockets for matches as he began to shiver from the night air. He felt through every pocket in his trousers and found two matches. He gathered some dry twigs and old leaves to start his fire, but when he lit the first match against the seat of his pants, the match broke in two pieces. The fire end flew into the rubbish and went out. Carefully, he pulled out his last match. He cussed his luck for being so clumsy and for getting lost. He lit the match, and the dry leaves soon began to burn. When he was sure that the twigs were well started, he began to make a big fire, piling on any chunks of dry wood he could find. When the night grew darker, his light shone high in the sky, and he hoped someone would see it. His rifle stood beside a half-burned log, and he sat down with his back against the old charred windfall.

He was worried. Curly told me it is ninety miles to the mountains, he thought. So far, I haven't been able to see them. I wonder if I'm in the unsurveyed territory, or will I find the railroad track and get to a town? He sat for a while longer and began to feel the heat from his fire.

About midnight, Big George was still awake. He wondered if I was out looking for him yet. These boys will tear the woods apart to find me, he reassured himself.

Suddenly, he heard a noise in the brush. He reached for his rifle and sat quietly beside the heat of the fire. In another minute, he saw a large moose walk into the firelight. It stood a few minutes, rubbing its head and neck against a tree. The rifle was in the big boy's hand. He was lost and hungry. Oh, how he wished for a larger rifle. Liver toasting in the coals would look awfully good to a hungry man. Then fear took over. People talk about ferocious animals like bears and wolves, he thought, but a wounded moose is the most savage of all. Big George sat still and did not shoot. In a couple of minutes, the moose walked away into the night.

All four of us riders spread out, in formation, about a mile wide. We rode with the light of the fire behind us. We circled the black alder, calling the big fellow's name and giving out a war whoop at intervals. From each high point, we looked for a campfire, but saw nothing.

I was thinking about my old friend. Accidents can happen very easily. Maybe the old boy has tripped on a root and fallen onto his rifle. It could have blasted a hole the full length of him. He may have tried to get a drink from the creek and fell in headfirst, or he could have been attacked by a bear. If he shot at a bear with that small rifle, it would eat him alive. The other riders were thinking similar thoughts.

It took hours to go a few miles through such country in the night. We rode until the light from the brush pile became so dim that it was unsafe to go farther. If Big George had gone this direction, we surely would have seen a light from his fire. When we came together, we decided that he must have come across a house where somebody lived and visited until it was too late to leave.

We spread out, coming back on different ground. When we reached the creek near home, it was almost daylight. The brush piles had all been burned, and Dan and Seth were glad to see us return.

Whalebone sliced a few pounds of his roast meat, and we all had a feed. No one around this horse ranch slept a wink. The night had been cold, and we had worn chaps and heavy coats. We thought about our old friend in shirt sleeves and felt chilly.

The sun came up bright and clear, but to me it seemed to have risen from the wrong direction. I said, "That's the first time I've ever seen the sun come up there. What direction will it set tonight? If I couldn't see Chin Whiskers so easily, I'd never be able to leave camp. It's no wonder Big George didn't get back yesterday. Too bad he didn't know about that high peak. I think we better scout around the settlement again this morning. If he didn't hole up with someone, we had best get everybody out on the hunt for him today."

"When a person is lost," Dan said, "it's supposed to be reported to the RCMP. I'll take the Ford and go into town and phone the police. They'll come right out here, organize a hunt, and stay until he's found."

As Rawhide rode out to wrangle some more horses, I told him, "Bring all the gentle ponies you can find. Some of these settlers know this country, and some will want to ride a horse. We can take the roughest end of the string if we haven't enough to go around. Seth has gone to root out the settlers, and Dan has gone to notify the police."

By six o'clock, Rawhide was back with a bunch of horses. I opened the gate and helped corral them. "How many ponies can we ride out of the lot?" I asked.

Rawhide closed the gate and climbed to the top of the corral to look over the horses. "I must have about all the saddle stock here. I can count twenty-three that we have been riding at one time or another. How many neighbours do we have?"

"I don't know," I answered, "but if we could get ten men mounted who know the country and have them spread out in formation like last night, they should find something, dead or alive. Maybe I'd better go on foot and look for tracks. I'd know Big George's track if I saw it in Africa."

All the neighbours soon got together at Seth's house and planned strategy. Some wanted to ride a horse, but most preferred to walk through the woods. I walked down the trail toward the brook with the long culvert and soon picked up Big George's trail. I saw where he had taken a drink by the culvert and where he had walked a few steps away from the creek. I also spotted the tracks he left when he had stood beside the wagon and talked to Seth. All day, I followed his trail and discovered where he had rested on a log and then started down the hill. But I could never follow the tracks for more than a few steps without losing them again.

Just before sundown that night, I found Big George's tracks leading to the log house with the padlock on the door. He had obviously stopped several times around the doorway, went around the house, then left the clearing. This made hard tracking, but it was enough to show me the direction he had taken and to know that we had been searching in the wrong area the night before. I hunted another hour, finding tracks and losing them again. Tired and almost discouraged, I walked across the creek to Lock's place and followed a narrow trail home.

The riders were home early, and Whalebone was feeding the lot cowboy-style as they sat around the log cabin. I found my saddle and put it on a fresh horse before I had my supper. Listening to the riders talk, I learned they had not been well organized and had crossed each other's tracks. I was sure this would happen again. I thought, If I don't find Big George tonight, I'll head that party again early in the morning.

The cut line that passed the lake was carved out for more than ten miles. All the stumps had been removed, but no road had been built. An Indian trail from Kelly Lake wound back and forth, crossing this cut line many times. I figured that if Big George had walked in a circle, chances were that he had turned left. If he went left, he may have found the cut line, and instead of coming home, might have walked in the wrong direction. The cut line was not more than a mile to the left of where his tracks left the log house.

After I finished supper, I filled my pockets with matches and started out for Kelly Lake. I shouted "George" as loud as I possibly could. Each time the Indian trail crossed the cut line, I lit a match and looked for footprints of a big man. I went like this for ten miles to Kelly Lake, without seeing a track. As no one lived along this cut line, no one heard my calls to the lost man.

When I returned to Seth's house, it was somewhere between midnight and daylight. The floor of the house was covered with so many sleeping bags that I could scarcely get in. The night had been cold, and I hoped that wherever the old fellow was, he wouldn't be cold or hungry. I rolled into a bunk beside Whalebone and said to myself, I'll rest until daybreak. I may not be able to sleep, but in the morning I'll head that crew of riders out of here as soon as we can see.

When Big George left his fire on Monday, he knew that he had no more matches and that the best thing for him to do was to stay by his fire, but he was so hungry. He walked to a high point of ground and looked around. Everything looked the same. He didn't know which way to head. He climbed over windfalls, dodged clumps of black alder, and kept on walking.

"If only I could find the creek," sighed Big George. He had not been able to find water, or any small game to shoot. Hunger slowed his steps as he tramped all day Monday with no idea of where he was. At night, he nearly froze. He wondered again where I was and called my name many times. His voice echoed in the woods and came back to him.

He thought about death. Big George was a brave man and would give his life for a friend or good cause, but he did not like to think of starvation. "If I only had water," said the lost man. "Oh well, I must never give up. Curly will find me yet. This is hell for the boys' first day in British Columbia." He thought of many things in his past, but nothing compared with being lost, hungry, and without water.

On Tuesday morning, I had a short talk with each rider who had been out on Monday. I tried to find out where they had been in their search for the lost man. I also talked to the men travelling on foot and told them where I had last found the big fellow's tracks. "We'll all start from those last tracks. We have the direction he left. I'm going to ride a horse, and I'll put ten men spread out in formation. We better keep close enough to hear each fellow shouting. You fellows who know the country well can turn us all back in time to get out of the woods tonight."

I was terribly worried. A manhunt in the woods of an unsurveyed region of northern British Columbia was a new experience for me. My mind took me back a few years to the time when a little girl was lost on the open prairie. I had saddled a horse and ridden all night until she was found. That was in open country with just some wheat sheaves to hide her. We should have an airplane here, I thought.

I led the ten riders to the log house and showed them the big tracks. "Now we'll spread out," I said, "but not more than a quarter of a mile apart. I'll take the outside circle. When I shout and the second man hears it, he shouts and the third man hears it. Keep this up all the way down the line. By doing this, each rider will keep within hearing distance. We'll all know where we are. We'll go as far as we dare, and before it gets dark, we'll circle and come out on the cut line. This way, we'll all have a chance of getting home."

The horses and the riders had a difficult time travelling through this terrain. The brush was heavy, and the horses had to climb over old fallen trees that had been rotting for years. I shouted until my voice was hoarse. My old friend was constantly on my mind. I bet he has called more for me lately than I can imagine, I thought. If we don't find him today, he's dead for sure. I can't understand why the Pouce Coupé police haven't arrived. If we don't find Big George today, they'll sure as hell hear from me. What do they think is important business, anyway? That old man is a real one. If I were lost, he'd never quit hunting for me. I'm afraid he's had an accident.

Sometime near noon, I could not hear any shouting from the rider closest to my right. I wondered why and swung in that direction, shouting continuously. I was thinking how easy it would be to get lost if we didn't cooperate. After several minutes of hard riding, I heard some men talking. Thinking that they might have found Big George, I urged my horse even faster. I came to a small lake, covering about twenty acres, with a very boggy outlet near the shore. Here, I found three riders with their horses bogged to their saddle blankets. My temper got hot in a hurry when I saw this. Loss of sleep and worry can do a lot to a man sometimes. I said to these three men, "It's bad enough to have to pull a muskeg, but it's a hell foolish thing for a man to ride a horse into one on purpose when he could have easily went around."

Much valuable time was lost here. I was sure that if I had not come to their rescue, the three men would have walked home, and the three good ponies would have been lost in the mire.

Again that afternoon, not long before sundown, I could hear shouting to my right. Discouraged and disheartened at thoughts of sundown and another day lost, I pulled my horse over to investigate. I found that the men who had been walking had come together to make plans to return home. They called all the riders together to count heads and make new plans. Everybody was sitting on an old dead tree, watching the last rays of the sun and talking. I did not dismount, but sat quietly for a minute, listening for new orders from the men on foot.

When the sun went down on Monday night, Big George thought he was going to freeze. As well as wishing for food and water, he now wanted a fire that would chase the chill from his weary bones. He was dog tired and had to rest, regardless of the cold, so he sat on the ground and leaned back against a tall stump—but only for a few minutes. He had to keep moving to keep his blood circulating. Without a coat, the night air was unbearable, and he had to get up often and swing his arms to warm his blood.

When daylight began to break, he started hunting for home once again. Before the middle of the day, Big George was tripping on everything. He thought to himself, I'm no closer to home now than I was yesterday. I know that I'm stumbling and making poor time. My eyesight has failed me terribly. I won't last another night without a fire and something to eat. I wonder where Curly is right now. I hope he knows I'm lost. If I only had a drink and some matches, I'd try to hold out until he finds me. If I don't find home today, this will be my last roundup.

I sat on my horse, looking in the direction that Seth was pointing. He was giving instructions to the men, who were ready to leave the log. Suddenly, Seth put his hands to his mouth in such a fashion that his voice sounded like a monstrous trumpet.

There was a faint answer from out in the brush. Without a word, I put my spurs to my horse and galloped in the direction of that feeble sound. I charged through brush that ordinarily would have scraped me from my horse. The horse jumped over old logs and windfalls like a hurdle jumper while I called "George!" at the top of my voice.

As I galloped, I heard another faint call. Still shouting loudly, I pushed my horse onward. I began to wonder if this call might be from another man on the hunt who had not met with the rest of us. I had not taken a count to be sure. I thought I heard other riders crashing through the brush behind me. Excitement was running high as I looked across a small valley about three hundred yards wide. On a burned-over patch of ground, I saw a man leaning against a black, charred stub of a tree. "Thank God, my prayers have been answered," I breathed. "There's the old boy . . . what's left of him." I dismounted in a hurry, and, speaking Big George's name, I shook his hand.

"I knew you'd come, Curly. I was afraid it might be too late, but I've been looking for you. I've just about had it, Curly. Do you know where we are? I can hardly walk any more. I need water."

"I just crossed a little stream of fresh water," I told him.

The big fellow's shirt sleeves were still rolled to his elbows. His arms were black from burned, charred trees and stubs, and his face was dirty and nearly black from whiskers and grime. His eyes were sunk way back in their sockets, and he had a glazed look. He clutched the small rifle in one hand.

I placed one of Big George's arms over my shoulder to support him and said, "Come on, big boy, we'll get a drink. Seth has a little lunch for you about half a mile back."

I led my horse and walked my old friend to the brook. "Don't take more than three good swallows of water," I told him. "A big drink might give you cramps and that could finish you. The boys have some water with them. You can take three more swallows when we get back to them, and then you can have lunch."

Two more riders arrived to help me lift the weak man onto my saddle horse. When he was loaded, he laid flat over the saddle horn. He rode that way while I led the horse and held onto the big fellow's leg to support him. When we arrived at the log where the men had been resting, they cheered and shouted with joy. Eva's jar of soup was relished by the exhausted and hungry man.

Night-time was upon us as the tired, but happy, crew of "manhunters" trudged for home in the dark. My feet were skinned and blistered from walking my horse home over such terrain. I followed my brother, Seth.

We arrived at Seth's log house about nine o'clock on Tuesday night. The crowd soon emptied the sourdough crock, finished pounds of roast moose, and drank gallons of coffee. Even Big George seemed to get over his hunger.

Eva prepared a good bed at her place for Big George. She gave him more broth and warm drinks and said, "I'll take over now. I'll feed him light until he's well enough to get back on his feet. I hope he doesn't get pneumonia from his exposure. Would someone find his pipe and tobacco? I'll provide the matches." Big George would sleep in a real bed that night.

More than a week later, the police from Pouce Coupé drove their car into Dan and Eva's yard. They asked Eva if the lost man had been found.

The men were all out working so Eva and Big George were alone. Eva answered, "Yes, the man has been found, but it was no fault of yours that he was. I'd like to know why you didn't come out here when he was lost as we expected you to."

The police just smiled at her and said, "You'd better put a bell on his neck when you turn him loose again."

After a few days of Eva's nursing, good care, and delicious food, Big George began to revive. His eyes did not seem to sink back so far and he gradually returned to good health.

Toward the end of the week, I had a chat with my old friend. He was thinking seriously of coming back to the prairie with me in a few days. He said, "You're the only man in our crew that is really tough and hardy. Most of us squawked plenty when the chuck wagon was lost, even for one night. You used to think that Rawhide and I were tough guys away back along the trail when we would get banged up with a horse. There was nothing to that. It was just our job. We couldn't begin to stand up to you after your luck. Things sometimes look far worse than they are, but this experience was bad enough to suit me or you."

"The Family" in 1944. Curly, Marlene, Jack, Jean, and Lena. *Courtesy Marlene Davidson*

Soon Big George recovered enough to start work. He sharpened his axe and began helping the boys build some log houses. Each morning when the big fellow got out of bed, he looked toward a certain high hill instead of watching the sun come up. Big George knew that from now on, his guide would be the huge hill with the large clump of spruce trees, known to all as Chin Whiskers.

Big George was feeling more like the old boy who had built our campfires along the trail. When Little Bill made music, Big George was ready to step-dance or sing, thinking how nice it was to be alive and among friends. He was once again telling jokes each day as he used to do.

"Big boy," I said, "when I get to be your age, I hope to have a dozen grandchildren. I'm going to tell them all about the old wrangler who could go so many days without food or water."

Before I returned to the prairies, I made arrangements to purchase horse feed for the winter blizzards. I traded some horses to my brother-in-law for the Model T Ford coupe, which I planned to drive back home.

I was ready to drive to Hythe to buy some oat sheaves and straw stacks when Big George came up to me. "I'm on my way to Hythe," I said. "Maybe you'd like something for snake bite. What do you say?"

Big George replied, "Curly, you know me so well. That's my weakness. This time, I'm going to say no. I'm not a drinking man from now on. Thanks."

The weather was favourable, and the work was under control. Whalebone had nearly filled the meat house with moose meat for the winter and still had prospects for a bearskin rug. Oat sheaves and straw piles were purchased at Hythe for the stock. All hands were anxious to see me get back home to my wife and daughter before all the ferries were taken out of the rivers.

On Monday morning, I bid them all goodbye. I gave Eva a bear hug and stepped into the Ford for the long journey to Val Marie. The crew of wranglers gathered around the car and all wished their old foreman a safe journey.

Rawhide shouted, "Write to us when your little cowboy is born. I'll send him a present." He continued, "We'll be expecting you back in the spring. Come in time to help us brand our colts."

Epilogue

THE HORSE RANCHES IN THE NORTH DID NOT BECOME A reality.

Big George returned to Quebec in the early thirties and died shortly after.

Whalebone died in the forties while working for a farmer in the North. He developed respiratory problems caused from treating seed wheat for smut. He never married.

Little Bill was also unfortunate. In the early thirties, he lost his life at a very young age from blood poisoning in his leg.

Rawhide returned to his father's ranch near Val Marie and continued to ride broncs and farm. In later years, he retired in Gull Lake, Saskatchewan, where he spent the rest of his life.

Curly's G Half Diamond ranch grew with Hereford cattle. In 1960, Jack and Irene Gunter took over the ranch. Curly and Lena retired in Ponteix, Saskatchewan, and Lena died in 1968. Curly lived among his many friends until his death in 1980.

Curly often said that the reason these cowboys never made it in the North was because they were prairie chickens, not bush rabbits.

Curly in 1963, riding Patches. *Courtesy Marlene Davidson*

(Left to right) Bill, Seth, and Curly Gunter in 1972. *Courtesy Marlene Davidson*